COLLECTED POEMS

CITY NATURE:

Collected Poems

WILLIAM CORBETT

JANE'S BOOK
CHRISTMAS '84!
All love,

Bill

The National Poetry Foundation
University of Maine at Orono
Orono, Maine 04469

Published by The National Poetry Foundation
University of Maine at Orono, Orono, Maine 04469

Printed by The University of Maine at Orono Printing Office

Library of Congress Catalog Card Number: 84-71923
ISBN: 0-915032-45-7 cloth
ISBN: 0-915032-46-5 paper

Beverly　　Marni　　Arden

ACKNOWLEDGMENTS

No poet who has published exclusively, as I have, with small presses arrives at a Collected Poems without the encouragement, care and attention of a few people. In my case these people are James Randall, Stratis Haviaras, Phil Zuckerman, Lewis Warsh and Bernadette Mayer, Lee Harwood and Jud Walker, Ric and Ann Caddel and Tony Baker. I am grateful to one and all. Joe Brainard, Philip Guston, Trevor Winkfield, Robert Nunnelley, Neill Fearnley and Jon Imber made covers for these books and pamphlets, and I thank them. And I take my hat off to those editors in whose small magazines many of these poems first appeared.

NO MATTER WHAT

A friend here had remarked recently that when he was in school, the proverbial one-room schoolhouse, in fact, they were taught to identify the local wild flowers and plants by means of large placards, the reproduction of the plant on one side, and the data relating on the other. So one could therefore walk out into a specific world of a shared and common information. Despite the fight now to save the environment, which word shares with 'world' a very wide application, there is little place indeed one is taught so to recognize and admit, to know by those ageless means of "habits and haunts," in Charles Olson's phrase, the particulars of where one physically is.

D. H. Lawrence had early nailed the wistful American aggrandizement of nature in his note on Crèvecoeur in *Studies in Classic American Literature*: "NATURE. I wish I could write it larger than that. N A T U R E. . . ." Such 'nature' is, of course, confined to the country and goes along with bears and bobcats and blueberries. But this is *City Nature*, what another artist of William Corbett's habits, Claes Oldenberg, had argued was just as actual as the rural kind and being intensively the fact of human nature, finally far more interesting.

The skills of this poet are so quietly and firmly established in his work that one is apt to forget about them in either reading or hearing—which is, of course, their mastery. If one takes as gauge the following proposal of Zukofsky, then the genius becomes apparent:

> How much what is sounded by words has to do with what is seen by them, and how much what is at once sounded and seen by them crosscuts an interplay among themselves—will naturally sustain the scientific definition of poetry we are looking for. . . .
>
> ["Poetry"]

Corbett's factual love for words, his trust that they will say his mind and feeling, that they literally matter, is profoundly engaging:

Christmas
A sleigh's wooshing hush
running fresh
jolly comice pear wobbles
on the table   white bells
let nothing you dismay

["Montpelier Biscuit"]

Nor has any poet more fixed a place in language, called it to be there as all that knowing it, and recalling, and having a life, lives, there, with all that these mean and have to mean—all that that ever can be. "February 29th," for one instance. Or the complex "Runaway Pond"—or "Vermont Apollinaire":

I cannot carry a tune
Not in a bucket one note. . . .

Whatever it is that poetry asks for, what it needs to survive and to be listened to, I can hear or see none of it without a human pattern, that stain or wear or humor or fear that it not last, that makes things said a hopeful enterprise, a whistling in the seemingly endless dark. Much like the story of the boy walking through the graveyard, who sings because he is afraid, I need a company, even my own voice if there is no one else's. But how dear to hear another's! What relief to know that someone is truly there.

Robert   Creeley
Waldoboro, Me.
July 3, 1984

CONTENTS

ANTHEM

for Ives' 100th Birthday

Milton Avery Altmar
Charles Burchfield Ashtabula
Harbor homesick Lucy
Sprague Mitchell Palo
Alto Claude Mench
East Mauch Chunk
Helen Lyles Greensboro
Arthur Dove Canandaigua
William Corbett Boston
Massachusetts Trumbull Connecticut
Easton Pennsylvania Danbury
Connecticut East Mauch Chunk
Pennsylvania Norfolk Virginia
Marni Arden Sean
Lucy Timothy Jennifer
cops and robbers
in the barn in the block long
black 1939 Packard
lake road blue sky
Judith Walker Brighton
England Gloriosa Daisies
spread over the hillside
Geraniums Fuchsia Begonias
hay mowed turned
Alexander Herzen tremendous
though nights are cool
children sleep warming
each other covers on the floor
Carleton "Pudge" Fisk Raymond
New Hampshire out for the season
lightning helps the corn grow
William Corbett Greensboro
Vermont Boston Massachusetts
slowly boats fishing
Jeffrey Greene two rainbow trout
green like ferns in shade
yellow as a robin's beak
sky blue enough for
a Dutchman's pants sun

13

shining to beat the band
purple Dahlias about
to burst noon shape
of an apple halved
cold and white Charles Demuth
look at the corn and peaches
Daisies Tomatoes Marigolds
clouds light blue sky
over Stannard Mountain
pasture look at that

TRANSLATIONS FROM THE CHINESE

Wet grass barefeet chill
spiderwebs in the short grass.
mind unable to leave well enough alone.
Will my sadness never come to its end?

Each morning surprised to find
this is not a dream. Still here
dreaming that I will wake
and begin to pack and leave.

Sheets tangled under me.
Stars hidden south wind
too sweet and damp.
Orange cat at the screen.

Finally white snow pea flowers
yellow cucumber blossoms earth
wet enough for weeding clover
and witch grass. Mindless pleasure.

Naked shivering on the rocks
Northern lights stars so bright
dazzle city eyes riotous night
drinking and dancing out of our heads.

Hung over sleepy head.
Blue blue sky far away
out the window. Too sore
to leave the pillow and rise.

Boys peer down stalking
move slowly no splashing
no clatter gathering crayfish.
A breeze stirs the water.

"Fame and money mean
nothing to me." Ha!
A mirror for integrity.

Nasty birds crows
atop pine trees
early morning fog
white wet powder.

How do they know
July's end blackeyed susans?
Time to leave
when asters bloom.

Whiskey, wine, beer
tonight. Expected sleep
I don't want to go home
wherever that is.
August before you know it.

Morning the earth steams.
Asparagus fern crystal
summer's ruin not just yet.
The hills are still, mindful.

POEM

Some black cloud in life
following us the rain blurs
our country things leap out
demanding our attention all at once.
I brought you this letter
although it was addressed to 8
which I crossed out and wrote 9
because this letter is addressed to you
the boy slept through the strangling
the children slept through the burglar's
tying their parents to kitchen chairs
the boy found his mother dead.
He was wearing a brown cap
stuffing envelopes in the library
one of the envelopes to a woman
whose husband wrote "addressee moved"
knowing she had moved to the next block
he wants custody of his kids
fears for their cleanliness and safety
"Does she fuck in front of the children?"

THREE, FOUR DAYS

Friends, policemen and immigrants
    cocaine
invisible but nice bones
ugly shoes and shovel hands
standing outside in the rain
                    died
on the train Monday
on the way home.

END OF APRIL

Night after thunderstorm
dogwood petals, creamy tulips
bashed to the pavement
blossoms scattered gleam.

Old love new nerves
silence wears thin.
Hopeless to be born
what arms open
in a grin? Spring
no simple profit.

Sweep up fallen
lavender tree flowers

ST. PATRICK'S DAY

Snowplows rumble March thunder
tomorrow New York
is today on the bus.
St. Patrick's Day four days
before spring a deep snow fell.
Clear blue sky storm's aftermath.
I remember waking to unexpected deep snow
beginning spring vacation prep school
two years in a row. Two weeks later
returned the grass green the willows
yellowing. The sky's blue bleached
drab in the tinted bus window.
Often the past two grinding
winter months I have felt
comfortable with myself finally come
to a way of seeing myself
that fits. *If* being a poet is
the conviction you will make poems
no matter what and ambition
but no expectations. A willingness
to accept the poem's accumulation
at the edge of the mind and not
demand the act define you
anew each time. As I write
my sense grows that I come
up short of what I feel
when I feel these intimations
of what I am and seldom pause
to dwell on them, savor instead.
This is New York. I read here
tonight from the black binder
three fingers work of a decade.
New York St. Patrick's Day not
in thirteen years come from college
to raise hell drunk. Glennons.
Clavins. Third Avenue bars tin ceilings
marble floored johns. In one, seeing
Charlie Conerly at a urinal
invited my friends to meet him.
Waking in a parked car Washington Square
the driver's coat on fire. Rode a motorcycle

through the Hotel Taft. That is the he
whom I know but no longer feel.
These charms I carry and declare:
armless open mouthed rubber gorilla,
gold earring, bottle librium, Arden's
black painted clay heart left pocket—
Guard me, the bright daylight
drifts past the clouds.

COLUMBUS SQUARE JOURNAL
12 OCTOBER 1974 - 12 OCTOBER 1975

Autumn sherbert
Yellow pansies lake warmed
        brown faces
Brussels Sprouts Swiss Chard
Vermont cheddar Molson beer
Caterpillar coat thick for cold
Punky watermelons white rotting cucumbers
        Parsley!
Summer past city clothes leather jacket, hat
Marni and Arden drawings
three years old save them someday

15 October

Purple petunias
into October
in the window

18 October

Horse tail clouds
scratches on the blue
setting sunlight on brick

                *

Blue twilight sky
streetlights white circles
fall   Magritte

20 October

Believe you me
no soap

Single oak leaf
a hand blown aimlessly
over the highway

Connecticut meadows
Connecticut stonewalls

BALTIC. OCCUM. BOZRAH. YANTIC.

INDIAN PRAYER

Who lives
in the Hotel Elton
who drinks
in the Legion Bar & Grill
walks a mile
in my moccasins.

INVENTORY

Two Rolling Rocks
Two Player's Navy Cut
One box Diamond matches my brother-in-law claimed
the white tips could make a bomb
The New York Review of Books
A pipe
One mother grandmother great grandmother living one
grandmother missing two grandfathers dead one grand-
mother near blind alone dying in an old age home
called a manor with a wishing well in its foyer
"The facts are nothing but propaganda"- Molotov
I remember he wore round rimless glasses
The mole to the left of my nose in the same place as
the mole to the left of Henry Ford's nose
Seven shirts one pair of pants at the cleaners
One spelling mistake so far

Three letters one postcard written earlier
Eighty-five cents on the marble mantlepiece upstairs
One letter to answer from a man I don't know
Six boxes of Fire Exits at the post office
another box of Fire Exits downstairs
An empty box of Player's for Joe Brainard
if he wants it
Two BE A TECHNICIAN match books
A.R. Ammons *Sphere* new long poem bought
at the Gotham Book Mart unable to afford
Ned Rorem's *The Final Diary* Ten Dollars
A headache last night and this morning work-
men using jackhammers on Columbus Avenue
Two politicians on television
Six plants one red telephone one empty
can Foster's Lager birthday present
Eleven days thirty-two years old
Three grey rugs various sizes from a garage
in Connecticut
Rug from grandmother's house in Pennsylvania
in the cellar tomorrow in the alley garbage can
12 pm
Fear of heights at Nichols' ledge Hardwick
Vermont two years ago
Two postcards in yesterday morning's mail
Dishes pots wok wine goblets glasses
garlic press forks knives spoons ladle large spoon
frying pan in the kitchen sink
A bee sting on Hillary's wrist
Two meetings or three tomorrow
Third floor light across the way goes out
Five cars the last one May '74
Three summers in Vermont
Not one phone call tonight
One ring, ink pen, leather jacket
pair of suede shoes
A Ray Kass watercolor an Arthur Yanoff painting
Oxford Dictionary
Bottle Evan Williams bourbon Carole King record
Twenty-four Charles Ives Records
One nightshirt birthday present
Four children on the steps singing
"La Cucaracha A Cockaroacha"
One attempt at spelling "La Cucaracha"

Fifty extra units on the TV
One marriage one friend East 10th Street New York
One sweet basil plant surviving from the summer
One brother on Linda Street San Francisco
One mother forever one father for twenty-three years
One right shoe with a hole in its sole
Some friends in upstate New York a dozen students
lock on the door box of old newspapers
No busing incidents yesterday
Two children asleep one father awake one mother studying
Hundreds of plywood windows in the John Hancock
black in the moon's light
Stoned smashed blotto whacked out pie eyed crocked
shit faced wiped out plastered pissed bombed eleven
words for drunk
Some smoke
Nine or ten Square Deal Composition books empty
Another night's sleep another cold another October
morning another glass fermenting fizzy apple cider

                                                    24 October

October of incomparable
Aegean cloudless blue skies
shoals of clouds at dusk
some pink and lavender
others soft crimson

                                                    26 October

Walking Coughers
White Girls in Harlem

What does it matter
to be broke today
or nearly so

Shotgun wedding
peanut butter, bourbon, housefly
radiators whistle

30 October

SEX AND VIOLETS

Christmas Anemones

    The sky sullen
    vaguely like cardboard
    cold rancor

glum serum

Tyranny of tiny words   Some milk

Hallowe'en

Hunter's moon rose orange
in costume for Arden
smoky night the dew
on cars and the street
like slime

    *

Penniless someday.
Not worth a damn
sitting there
like bumps on a log.
Upset tummy.

Father, father
where are you among
what people who have
no reason nor purpose
to know the house you fled.
I have wiped my plate clean.

3 November

Father, Father
where are you among
what people having
no reason nor appetite
to know the house you fled
now a decade?
Awake and asleep
I have wiped my plate clean.

3 November

Orchids in the upstairs
wash basin

Kirin Foster's Dos Equis

4 November

Smell of sex
fingers lips wet
the edge worn away
roughhousing

*

Overnight ailanthus skinny branches
leafless whip the vague air
color of a shirt cardboard and perfect
inspiration for an ax murder or stay
in bed reading, drowse, wake
suddenly remembering you have to be somewhere
but you don't and ten minutes
sleep is delicious. Through the door into
a small room a smaller room after that.

                    *

Broke with a capital B
envious of Post Office clerks
accepting cash, making change.
Cash! What a lovely
sounding word, cash!
Endless pockets empty
culture of lower case e's
worms of dread and impotence.

                                                    5 November

"I would like to convince a few people that
nothing is simpler than what I have to say."
                              Francis Ponge

Finding a penny every day
bright beads of rain
sparkle on the windows

                                                    6 November

Free For All
Once And For All

                    *

The cup's plum lip
A light frosting of pimples
A froth of pimples

7 November

". . . the peculiar ways buildings end in the air. . . ."
                        Edwin Denby

This indian summer's soft blue sky
comfortable as a shirt fresh from the laundry
fills the space above Copley Square
the block between Dartmouth and Clarendon
where one building ends
in a green copper bannister

8 November

"Rusty" Calley Freed
"It was no big deal, Sir."
The Kent State National Guard
acquitted signs photographs
for souvenirs.
The war is over.

Armistice Day

Arden's angry tears
That's what! That's What!
Her drawings of pie faced women
with braids and hippo noses.

                ";. . sunlight,
next to that, starlight & the moon's face,
yes, & ripe cucumbers & apples & pears"
                        from Praxilla's Hymns

32

My own smell at mid-night
wrapped in quilts warm
and with what memories
will I seduce sleep?
Sleeping cougher frightens me.

12 November

As much time
in the dark
as in daylight.

*

The way we're walking
in this cold shower
They'll soon see how old we are

*

Winter branches candle smooth
dripping, bony wicked looking
rain the color of frost

13 November

That woman she might be mother
champagne haired, slouching against the building
on the block where Serge Chaloff's
mother once taught piano

16 November

Making out like a bandit
hand over fist

These Lacustrine cities grew out of loathing
On the secret map of the assassins
No changes of support - only
A people chained to aurora
It is better this year
Far from the Rappahannock, the silent
"Worse than the sunflower," she had said
Perhaps we ought to feel with more imagination
Keeping warm now, while it lasts
Yes, they are alive and can have their colors,
Hasn't the sky? Returned from moving the other
These decibels

18 November

"a grisly pale has settled. . . ."
                    Frank O'Hara

A gristly pale knucklebone

"Gracious living is the bastard of gracious thought"
                    Ray Ronci

19 November

Israelis at Beit Shean heave
the corpses of three Palestinian terrorists
and one Israeli case of mistaken identity
from a window to the ground below
where the bodies are stomped
and flogged with switches before
being burned on a pyre of branches
by the crowd.

Yellow orange shiny berries
hard as candy seen from the bus
Utopia Parkway Joseph Cornell
high above Cayuga's waters
New York necklace of winking
lights windows of the Hotel du Nord
tiny wonders trapped.

21 November

Three days after Lucy's birthday
nothing sent and jackhammers again
all over Columbus Avenue - five minutes more
just five the sweetest sleep saved
for last and if death comes
with such, etc. Some kind of record
the purple petunia in the bathroom
window still blooming and with it Vermont.
How cold there now?
Some kind of queer look the mailman
gives me as I answer the door in
my nightshirt nonchalant as always
except that one time at ten I gave
water to workmen naked.
From San Francisco "The Black Tarantula"
another installment of her novel
I Dreamt I Was A Nymphomaniac and a letter
from Michael "Or does too much get read
as it is?" Yes and no and not lately.
I'll shave and shower and saddle up
my western shirt with the stain on it
gift of Joe Newman and walk to school
stopping at Star Market for the last
fifty-five cent packs of Player's and then
to the Post Office to start the mail again.
I'll be thinking of Joseph Cornell I think
the movies somewhat and the price of things.

*

Cold rain. Simenon
weather. Maigret's lunch
skate in black butter.
The rain splashing, raw
shine of neon over the wet street
Mademoiselle Vague more like butchered
until snow fell sticking to the cars.

BEDS

    for B

The bed upstairs for seven years made for us in Hanover, Mass.
before that a queen size mattress on plywood on cinder blocks and
before that the mattress had a modern headboard that bed bought
impulsively in Cambridge. Our honeymoon bed in Vermont falling
into the middle, a PLAN AHEA$_D$ sign propped against the pillows
by Mr. Messier. The divorcees' bed in Sunset San Francisco broken
in on one side. Beds in Pennsylvania motels. In the apartment East
81st Street the bed wedged between a bookshelf and closet. In
Vermont single beds with grey and white plastic covered head-
boards under the eaves sleep alone all summer. Alone waking in a
tub the Hotel Barclay Rittenhouse Square Philadelphia. Motels -
London, Ohio a vibrator bed run by quarters - St. Louis, East
Moline, Murdo, South Dakota Elko, Nevada. Sleeping on a tent
floor Missoula, Montana - in college on a mattress beatnickery - at
the homes and apartments of friends now forgotten - in a railroad
flat New York Second Avenue - in January an unheated cottage
Horseleech Pond. Sleeping in London, Copenhagen, Frankfurt,
Rome, Florence, Venice, Nice, Clermont-Ferrand, Paris, on the
S.S. Berman, one night a lumpy straw filled mattress the Hotel du
Nord Vienne, France. Waking hungover the back seat of a car stiff
once on the New Jersey shore slate grey late August sky. The
green metal bunk beds of prep school. Sleeping on 110th Street
in New York "BIRD LIVES" written on the mirror, an opera
singer warming up next door, a busted water pipe stinking in the
closet. Sleeping in Center Street Jim Thorpe seven summers, in
the man's car returning from Brady's Lake. How many years in
the room at home with the cowboy, indian and cactus wallpaper?
At Bob and Gerald's the bed under the canopy waking in July and
February. In sleeping bags once or twice as a boy "sleeping out."

Waking not knowing where I was once in Easton, Pennsylvania in Spencerport, New York in a child's bed once in Trumbull, Connecticut in the new house with the family room and the closet's louvered doors I could not place. Sweet naps on the couch in the study in Vermont. Bad dreams in the nursery beds. Sleeping in Northwood Narrows, New Hampshire Hancock, Mass Lake Leelanau, Michigan on East 10th Street New York Livingston, Montana Herman Street San Francisco Dartmouth Street Boston. The bed in Old Greenwich across from your great grandparent's wedding picture. Sleeping in the homes of friends - the Braiders Danbury, Connecticut Cooperstown, New York Redding, Connecticut Clinton, New York. Sleeping on a church floor Washington, D.C. and before the march in 1970 in the suburban home of a man who drank martinis mixed in a silver milk can and worked for the C.I.A. and whom I still dream about. He's standing against a peach colored wall drink in hand talking to me. Sleeping almost always with a pillow, naked or with a nightshirt or the shirt I wore that day not pajamas since I don't know when. Waking to the cool fresh morning air after a snow fall in Vermont or Concord where horses pulled the sidewalk snow plows, in Connecticut, in Pennsylvania and tomorrow morning if tonight's snow sticks and holds in Boston my own big bed.

26 November

The moon was white
as soap as good
as cold November
long in the tooth
spoons cakes and crusts
of frost and snow

Bobby Leach - Dionne Quints - Executions - Toll Roads -
Novelties - Tortures - Nudes (no art) - Indian Chiefs - Ferries
Fantasy - Push Carts - Chastity Belts - Slavery - Negro - K.K.K.
Cross Country Walks - Opium Dens - Riots - Strikes - Crime -
Risque - Hangings - Hay Rides - Moonshine Stills - Sod Houses
Old West - Massacres - Mussolini - Blacksmith Shops - Garages
Gas Stations - Tong Dens - Gambling Dens - Pool Halls - Mission
Houses - Beer Wagons - Horse Drawn Wagons (Close Ups Only)
Ghettos - World War II - Boer War - Hindenburg Disaster - Tokyo
Earthquake - Child Labor - Horse Cars - Massachusetts Depots

Thanksgiving Day

Deserted holiday morning hours
suit me walking to Ray's studio
through my neighborhood's barrel chested
brick houses stout and staid
helped to poignancy under Thanksgiving's
somber grey and puffy clouds.
Winter holidays ought
to be this grey and chill
deepening the day's natural quiet.
Near South Station an eyeless
dead pigeon on the pavement.
South Station, I was here
on my way home from camp
twenty years ago never thinking
I would be here now
about to enter Hayes Bickford
and call Ray. Red and green jello
A thin shaking woman takes a
cigarette from her green plastic
case. Old men smoke here
which I find courageous
but sobering to imagine
myself old, alone smoking
some holiday or other thirty
years away. What happened during

all those days I promised myself
to note and look forward to
years ago so I might measure
my life and sit rapt
pondering how much I wanted
to know where I would be
as if a sure future
could order a difficult present?
Smiling Buddha cakes good luck
and good luck fish Chinese
bakery window I pass going
slowly home a different way.

30 November

WASHING BILL SAX BOWLS

Speckled gray smooth
belly of a lake trout.
Azure swirls, cerulean glaze
plum-rose smear runs
clear along the lip.
What a pleasing
affirmative heft
these bowls smoking
clean from the dishwater
blessed with a calm
and rightness bless us.

1 December

VALSE NOT

Transience of all things
mutability odes
ruins something any
thing two step.
In college

I had a teacher
he wrote a book
One Man's Meter
he sang Keats to
"You're the cream
in my coffee"
and advised me
"Read a good book
after dinner every night."

8 December

Shreds of pencil colored cloud
scratched on like rapid doodles
give way to a thunderstorm
queering again the chance of snow.

*

"I do not cross my father's
ground to any House or Town."

For her writing Emily Dickinson liked best the inside of used envelopes. Joseph Cornell sent a small box to the actress Sheree North but never heard from her. Paul Strand's father was the distributor for "Domes of silence" the little devices that keep chair legs from scraping on the floor. I was told Rolfe Humphries' father played on the same New York Giants' team as Fred Merkle, Christy Mathewson and Rube Marquard but there is no record. Charles Burchfield designed wallpaper for a long time in Buffalo, New York. "O the moon it spent a night along the Wabash / Through the sycamores it did shine" - Theodore Dreiser. William Faulkner worked on the screenplay for *Land of the Pharoahs* - Dewey Martin, Jack Hawkins and Joan Collins. Milledgeville, Georgia birthplace of Flannery O'Connor and Oliver Hardy. Charles Ives Deke and Libra. Dashiell Hammett and Lillian Hellman stayed for a time on the cuff in the New York hotel managed by Nathanael West. The postman in Torrington, Connecticut his house full of undelivered second and third class mail. The lady on Marlborough Street her house emptied of several dumpsters full of garbage by court order and three years later nearly thirty white

40

Borzois discovered cooped up there after neighbors heard the dogs' howl at night. The New York brothers crushed to death when the heaps of newspapers they had accumulated and arranged into a labyrinth collapsed on them. Constance, Glenda and Gordon locked in the attic for years by their parents lived on cookies, cereal and television. Emily Dickinson allowed her doctor to examine her through a half open door: Charles Ives "Connecticut Yankee" never read the newspapers and Joseph Cornell lived all his life on Utopia Parkway. A scar on Ives' finger. Emily Dickinson claimed she did not learn to tell time until she was fifteen. John Kane fought Jim Corbett to a draw and Ernest Hemingway boxed Wallace Stevens' ears. Djuna Barnes lives on in a Greenwich Village single room. She calls publishers printers. So many words. So much money. Seven from seventeen hundred and seventy five. Jonathan Edwards rode forth with bits of paper, his thoughts, pinned to his coat. CHARLES STARKWEATHER CHARLES WHITMAN RICHARD SPECK DUANE POPE. The Wayne Spelberg family of Racine, Wisconsin lived in the basement of his mother's home by candlelight one year. They went out only at night and ate the groceries his mother bought with money from a small inheritance. Spelberg's wife, seven months pregnant. "escaped" claiming she had been held against her will but her husband and children denied this. Vachel Lindsay mounts the stairs toward a bottle of cleaning fluid.

10 December

[1]
Nodding asleep sitting up
a desire to have what
might happen erased
Will I be drunk
on Friday night as you will be?
My head is on my chest
emptied. I want to . . . I want to
my head is in the hands
of sleep like having my life
stop and begin again when
it's all been said and done.

41

[2]
Rip Van Winkle
nodding asleep sitting up.
My head falls to my chest
an empty. My head in the hands
of sleep like having my life
stop and begin again when
it's all been said and done.

[3]
How dull How lifeless
How unlike himself
he's become
or he's apeshit, really
what's all this about going
to cut his finger off
for something it did last night?
Will I be drunk
as he wants me to be
on Friday?

11 December

Philip, I waited for your call
tonight glancing at the clock
as if I had to be somewhere on time
expecting any minute to hear you say "Are
you sure I won't be bothering
you? Are you sure you're
finished with dinner? Now
how do I get there again?"
Expected you to come and sit
at the other end of the kitchen table
smoking, drinking and talking.
What I had to say
is how much I like
the new drawings in the New York show.
That grizzled head smoking
his brow like a knuckle
the chair and lamp made

from bones I guess, my favorite
and the whipping man in his footsteps
shoes, a pyramid of shoes. Outside
a firecracker and yelling
Beverly calls from upstairs:
"Someone is shooting in the alley!"
I run out as if there were
something I could do about it
to find on West Newton Street
a hatless cop gun drawn
standing by his patrol car.
He's got "one," a black boy
his partner's chased the other
into the alley where a third cop
follows drawing his gun. More police
cars blue lights flashing. Beverly heard
"Wait, I'm only fifteen . . . Stop
or I'll blow your head off"
then the gunshot or two.
What you missed!

20 December

FOR MICHAEL PALMER

The woods were
russet when they
were not green The
grass orange or
sere or snowed
over white ponds
over birch trees
arched and slim

Mid-night
sweet roll & butter
Granny Smith apple
green empyrean.
Lemon juice, honey
bourbon, boiling water
hot toddy drink
it right off.

3 January

Reading Flaubert's letters
"we create imaginary troubles
for ourselves . . . we sow our own
path with brambles"
riding the bus
to Queen Anne's Corners
suddenly I know
I am happy with my life
joyous really this moment
Beverly we walked down
the street together
for the first time
in it seems months
crocheting in the seat in front.
Joyous passing by industrial
Boston white smoke
rising into grey clouds
passing over a weak
silver sun. CHINESE CHURCH
black block letters on white
Irish Riviera L Street
Brownies exalted steaming
chilled from the ocean's
icy water New Year's Day.

I gave up my husband
then my wife. He moved away
I walked out on her
got a writ, a lawyer
wrote out our live's garbage
not for love nor money.
The children looked after themselves.
I lived alone together
alone apart. He was a bully
beat me until I let
the world know. She was cold
without heart two years
out of eight we kept
going away we kept coming back
to piss and moan, to pick fights
getting close to cutting loose
from each other. White Red Black
Come then blood then ink.

Waking dread ten of nine
one spring couldn't find
myself in the mirror
the future caught up
with me. I sit and write
night owl every night
the tree of lights
wept through this morning's
light where steps of ice
stride and my mind
is less a cloud
now the arctic ring.

SHADOW TAG

Tired. I've been up
all day walking
on the outside of my feet
and half the night.
Read myself to sleep.

A ring around the moon headache
Chocolate covered pants yellow socks dirty feet
You're so brilliant you must write a book
Reading for instruction is fine but not for pleasure
It's nearly time to go to bed you must be tired
Three children with strep throat
The ball has a leak
Short division corner West Newton Street
Mind if I
Eyes like two holes in a blanket
A meal of vegetables
There was a man, no two men
Yellow turtleneck outside it in
Ghostly sneeze of the pollen air
When you get up wake me if it's not too early
Oops
That book this beer
That would be like taking a ham sandwich to a banquet
Eat some of your own shit
In bed with a bad haircut
You're cleaning up your eating habits I see
I'll stand for my brother and so will my father my uncle
    and my mother
Hold the smoke drink in
You're always sort of feeling your way
They all look like actors you can't quite place
Blonde girl with shiny lipstick
It's for your own good
The alarm rings before a closing
Do you have ear trouble or can't you hear?

After you've gone
Clear as ice I understand
What if sometime you have to do something you don't want to
    then where will you be

Cheap coincidence today riding my bike
down Boylston Street a man crossed in front of me
I thought he looked like you
but did not think of it again
until you called getting in touch
for the first time in three years.
Your wife and children, brothers, sisters
mother and father, your depression
of a summer ago you're drinking less.
My wife and daughters, mother and brother
a man we knew as a boy
named "Snake" now relaxes gardening
orchids, stealing exotic species from the Everglades
other friends seen rarely, a couple
not seen at all. What is there to say
and having little to say what bother
will it be remembering twelve years
ago drinking beer eating drunken eggs
in Pennsylvania or the night drunk we fought
on the stairs: a car crash Parsippany
New Jersey: soulful talks about each
other's character. Character? What did we
know then? I've forgotten, forgotten everything
we said but the earnestness
I remember. It's bitter cold here, in the teens
the air glittering like it must have then
coming drunkenly home to Spring Garden Street
the coal fire we never learned to properly bank
gone out our attic room freezing.
What's become of Dick
ex-MP, ex Life Guard who returned
after six years only to flunk out
broke he gorged peanut butter
after midnight thinking we were asleep.

Cuts like a hot knife
through butter wouldn't melt
in her mouth more flies
with honey than vinegar.
Thuds shut like a coffin
nail other peoples
or your own three
on a match homely
as sin two raisins
on a breadboard
sorer than hell teeth
eating an apple
through a picket fence
keeping your nose clean.

4 February

Dreaming I am in Nice
fucking this black haired girl
on the bed and the floor.
I step outside but this
can't be Nice these trees
and sloping meadowland, Vermont!
on a hill talking to a friend
while below us swimmers come
up from under the khaki
colored water of a man made
pond and bob under again.
The checks arrived this morning's mail.

8 February

I'd rather be running errands
hungover in Montpelier in July
than Boston February practically
skating over snow crusted sidewalks.

But I surely would not have argued
over abortion, history and the faces
of my family as the way
people ought to look
and I wouldn't be walking
with you Karin wondering if my face
is the one that will make other faces
in your world look real to you.
"Real" meaning, I guess, familiar
easy to read, if you're going to be
one who has the virtue
of trusting first impressions.
After all we only see each other
for the first time once. No, that's not true
for as you grow I'm seeing
you for the first time often
like Christmas day the hand written
book of poems made by you and Jenny
I didn't know anyone understood
so well what I do with my life
understood without making a thing
of it but a present yielding
something of myself as I wish to be known.

12 February

Right off the bat
smelling like roses
goes over big
the straight and narrow
Indian giver
hold your horses
shit or get off
the pot to your
heart's content keep
your shirt on from
a hole in the ground

What snow so
soft and grainy
heaps roughly made.
Large coleus
like a chandelier
leaves on the floor
on the book *T & G*
single leaf curled there.
Ash prints foreheads
white as snow
melting spots their
bare faces. They go
trampling, soaked
through the snow.

13 February

Turn blue like a hole
in the head drop dead
falling off a log hard
as rock hard as nails
big shot hearts in the right
places scarcer than hen's teeth

14 February

Valentine's Day
the same green shirt
worn out elbows
smiling through.
Phantom of the Clouds
in for breakfast
a comice pear
red like the cheeks of someone
just in from the cold
cut away the rotten spots
like life short of the sweet
succulent flesh.

Walking up and down
other people's sidewalks.
Tired people. Slack
overweight, their faces pitted
dark rings their eyes.
Shoe stores, bars
and churches.
The acid green
canal water.
Wide avenue, too wide
empty feeling.
Washington's Birthday shoppers
go about their business
buying clothes grocery store's closed.
The bars resemble blockhouses
narrow windows set shoulder height
someone can look out
it is difficult to look in.
In the alleys frame houses
poor ugly asbestos shingles
windows decorated with china
figurines, plates, plastic flowers
before the drawn shade.
March wind just behind
cold February. Come spring
blow the street dreck
clean, dry puddles away.
Since September
NIGGERS SUCK, Nazi signs
up to the heights
where Knox's cannon
brought from Ticonderoga
shelled the British
out of Boston
Evacuation Day.

February's end near
full moon's height
shine becalmed & fern
shadow on the wall.

Sore throat   rain
freak snow flakes
large as slaps
sunlight some time.
Buffalo marrow the trapper's butter.

A knock at the door
Rene Daumal stopped
in mid sentence, rose
answered the door
never to return
finding himself in a meadow
tickled by the cold
a thicket soon reached
the outskirts of a city
begun abruptly dark streets
people walking, wearing cheap clothes
smoking, talking people.

Lunatic: an animal somewhat
surrounded by jews,
Old Ez said, and heroine
she tricked allied troops
into a minefield to save Germans.

Pound's Doctor Kavka
laughed to hear
Confucius as a defense.
"Circumcision," Ezra said
"it must do something
after all those years
and years when the most
sensitive nerves in the body are. . . ."

17 March

St. Patrick's Day drinking
in Glennon's next to a man
with tiny green stars
pasted all over his bald head.
Mother's birthday. She says
her mother had a puss on
long as a wet week.

25 March

Five days before Easter in New York.
Easter Monday deKooning's painting
Mohammed's birthday death to King Faisal
cancelling the Arab proverb:
the face you know is better
than the face you do not know.
Maundy Thursday Good Friday Saturday
tinfoil chocolate rabbit wrappers
Marni's painted egg shell
yellow chicks with orange legs
occasional rain giving way
to snow flurries
and if there is thunder in March
March drunk with itself
wet nights, nights for mysteries
The Fire Engine That Disappeared
Martin Beck, Stockholm before sleep.

Waking Easter morning
soft grey morning grey like
the settling city dust
on windowsills and walls
waking on a couch
under the red slipcover
remembering New York
upper west side twelve years ago
friends not seen since when
wondering about the lives
of friends in the next room
theorizing about their life
pleasant to do half asleep
wondering, as always, if they love me
if I love them and what
our lives together hold for us.

1 April

Cold grey morning grey like
a smudge the sun
a spot of solder

5 April

Purples & butters snow crocus
cups, egg cups spear leaved
cold arthritic hands even
in the kitchen even young
pinky finger an arc that way.
What of the tulips, daffodils?
All thumbs? What of the skinny
nasty looking branch tips
and the damp ground smells?
Watermelons, radishes, daisies
packages . . . adults are bored Saturday.

BORED   MAGIC   DEATH

Between the Sheets
            also
Lonely Wives

lump heart
love's un-
realized, stopped
cold frame.

Walker Evans dead
the rooms empty out
many thousands gone
no survivors unseasonable spring.

Rossini toothless sucked pasta
died from gluttony.
Hunger makes head hurt
thinking also thinking out loud
spring makes this headache
heavy blossom carried drooping
everything happens at once
by itself - what the sun picks out
crocus purple and white
orange tongues short lived

buds their tiny yellows
pale fuzz on the albino's cheek
he's entering the subway
damp earth smells
from backyard shade
where freshly bloomed daffodils
yellow stars bend
toward the sunlight seldom there.

*

Billy Meyers. Billy
              Your mother
in her cotton apron
before the stove talking
to us over her shoulder.
I thought you were perfect
not just because my mother
complained; "Why can't you
be like Billy he's this
he's that he listens to *his* mother."
You seemed to do the right thing
instinctively while I cheated
or thought I did, stumbling
not sure what to say.
The last memory, crying
behind a parked car
after you told me
I could not hitchhike
to Bridgeport with the older boys.
This long to give that up.
              Peace, mother.

                                        22 April

How bright of me to live
in an age of full days, short poems
sweet clams   oranges   pizza.
This woman I walk beside
imagining my kiss stirring

the back of her neck
small of her back, hush.
What I don't know about her
What I will know about her
What she will know about me.
Love weakens me, tender butterflies
winking spring teenage blushes
red bliss hot but delicate
wonderfully slender thread.
Will Rodgers will win the Boston Marathon
we'll meet a man we like.
Triumphant the runners, exhausted
clasp hands as they finish.

3-4 May

The man without arms
The woman tearing paper into bits
The clock has the hands
The man without sleep
A dry retching: flannel or paper
Soapy glass of water in the dark
The woman at the door
The hands on the clock's face
The woman writing the man's hands asleep
He wants his daughter to call
and ask him to break both her
boyfriend's arms if he doesn't do something

6 May

Sitting talking thinking
about you walking thinking
about you these dogwoods
a blizzard or so   magnolia
blossoms falling apart
you never learn to talk
listening to the trees

you don't need to
thinking about you once
the workman smokes
a cigarette while he lifts
a manhole cover with his pick
thinking about you wildly
tonight seated here shaking
as if to jump out of my skin
into your skin? into
next week? or the life
I'll lead if we're ever
out of love?

7 May

You just fall in love
one day then you ask
"Will it ever be the same?"
The month of May, perfect!
What do you think
is going to happen is dim
but a consolation figuring
this month next year time
itself will have gathered things up
making a bouquet or night soil
of even my cigarettes
even your trembling arms
even my wanting to see you
right now

14 May

       "Satisfaction is a lowly
thing, how pure a thing is joy"
Flesh is fatal
satisfied this minute
anxious for the next
in all innocence.

Joy is too pure
a thing none are safe
who can't be satisfied.
If I could shut
my eyes and not see you.

18 May

What the old women
carry in their shopping bags
is sex, sex their underthings
and the old men
diet on Vietamin E, bone
meal and royal jelly.
In the country there are
tattoos "BUCK" on her
upper arm "MARY" on his
under a pair of dice
coming up seven.

*

A large sleigh bed
not because we're drunk
in the dream after
"The Postman Always Rings Twice"
I can't reach you
with what I must say
bitten by black flies
pinks yellows apple tree
spill white blossoms
water seeps everywhere
through the low places
I carry you
in my heart spilling over.

The man beside himself
The woman in another state
Smoking wide awake painting man
The woman types the pileated woodpecker at the stump
The man below the woman outside
his head in the woman's hands
drowning man's head the water clocks
The young man with a pillow
in front of his chest self portrait
his head full his own big bed quick
which once meant alive
not like the telephone like the bacon legs
other morning's other nights
The man's fat brick city
The woman napping on the couch
her mouth open dreaming
The man beside himself

27 May

Everything is technology: ice tongs and orchids
like shit through a tin horn there are mechanical ways
after the horse chestnut seeds scattered on the street
the rain spots the sidewalks suddenly drenches the city
standing water in gutters waits its turn.
When the mechanics are completed dreaming was better
you might wish the characters but in the story
you leapt upon her on the pavement naked, like that!
a swan dive in without a splash
sledding over the slippery streets wet and rough.

29, 30 May - 1 June

"We thought the ice
would never go out
this year but maybe
we began to look for
it to leave too early."

*

"I cut logs and my hands
are a helluva mess because
I'm allergic to the sap.
And I love to fish but
wouldn't eat one for anything."

*

Few apple blossoms sad to miss their fall

*

Purple, pink and lunar white
dandelion roots turned up
and raked from the garden.
Underground *is* another world.

*

"If those plum trees are alive
they're keeping it to themselves."

*

Apples - Duchess Wealthy

*

Single monarch butterfly
over the garden
day dreaming of you.

*

"My wife wants one thing.
My son wants another
his friend wants another.
I don't know what I want."

*

Dirty lukewarm bath water
reading Turgenev's *Hunting Sketches*.
A collarless white shirt
yellowed buttons, worn red
corduroy pants dress for dinner.

4 June

One day what it was
was a warm breeze
now passed, a love tap.

8 June

Stepping from the movies
into the cool June streets
turning toward the summer
of our future in Barcelona
and why not? or Paris
the way it looked
one night in the rain
on Commonwealth Avenue the brighter
new street lights reflected
wetly on the pavement making
the tree's shadow fuller, relief
from the rain under the full trees
shivering and purring in each other's arms.

10 June

Ellen in her bathing suit
leaning against the hawthorn tree
all summer reading the Russians.

Usual pre-Vermont apprehension
tingling feet, hand wringing, white
impatiens like the flower that grows in shade
the fears that come by night
dim chance of sleep:
Corbett my name morbid my nature.
Poison. If I had the instinct
to leave it the way the cats
leave the pancreas of field mice
they kill and eat beside my bed
and forget the kitchen's full of knives.

16 June

Moon white clematis circles
the tree West Newton Street
circle me in your arms
the nights we sleep apart.

Bunker Hill Day

Pulling witch grass and dandelions
from between the patio's brick
before the study, remembered
when I stood here looking
at the night sky thinking of you
as you said I must "a special place"
and saw a ball of powdery light
like the sun through haze one minute
and nothing the next but to wonder.

                    *

"Looks like a ceiling
of blue water . . . feels like. . . ."
drifts over the lake from a rowboat

just after I gripped the rock
startled to find I had been asleep
and nearly slipped into the water.
A yellow pollen scum
on the water, some fish circles.
The sky hazy between
clouds which appear to be
rolling over themselves slowly
gaining northerly momentum.
I can crumble the rock's
ash colored lichen with my fingers.
Reading *Justine* Alexandria's lime dust, sex
feels like this caressing air.

18 June

YELLOW

A gust shakes
dusty yellow pollen
off the pine trees
onto the lake
washed thickly
upon the shore.
The bumblebee works
his yellowblack head
into the baby blue
bell like comfrey flower
for a moment goes off
off like twilight's scatter
flicked from the young
banana green ferns.
The moon behind
blue and black clouds
the kitchen's bug lights
like buttercups spread
over the pine planks.

I meant to press buttercups
clover, bunchberry, hawkweed
from that field into a book
for you to celebrate this moment.
The field is brilliant where the flowers
grow in clusters. Soon the hayrake.
Parting is renewal.

Ben - The day after
the longest day of the year
tired and pink as the sun
squares of its dying light
appear on the screen door
it sets behind the lattice work.
Drinking Oppenheimer Krotenbrunnen
remembering how you enjoy rolling
those German wine names
off your tongue as if savoring
in the operatic fullness
their fruity pleasures again.
Last night we drank
five bottles of Piesporter Michelsberg
Reisling through a long dinner
ending as the full moon
lay upon the lake water.
We danced in the kitchen
doing dishes wanting everyone
we love to be with us
a present for us all
something we treasure knowing
we empty this to fill
ourselves again from the same source.

Planting monkshood
and thistle
frais du bois every
where milk white
turning pink, ripe red
enough taste to whet
your appetite for more
and you see the berries
more clearly your fingers
pluck under their leaves
at the base of weeds
and brambles.

"A soft second light of dreaming"
such lovely damage
like the wild roses
damaged in a soft
way soon after blooming.
A lovely fall
to where I want to be
"sighs and wishes in ink."

Air surrounds us
at least you felt "inside"
rain surrounds us now
moving north to south
slowly blending hills and lake
in a gray like erasure.
What if you don't feel anything clearly
at moments like this? Not anxiety
or peacefulness nor even
some feeling vague as evening drifting

behind the rain below the sky
rift with a violent blue
where a rainbow might be expected.

4th of July

"Memory is a strange bell - Jubilee and Kneel"
Emily Dickinson

5 July

Dragon Chasing a Bull
with Silver Rain and Thunder
Monkeys Invade the Heavenly Palace
fireworks "the most beautiful power
in the sky that belongs to all the people"
a whistle
followed by a brilliant flash of flame
bonfire and rainbow illuminations.

6 July

Sitting, staring, obsessed
by the line of your mouth
drawn east where your feathers
melt and compress
a slow avalanche of flesh.
A mother of eight
father with a history of mental problems
death by accident, murder, policy.
Sitting, staring your face smeared
the entire distance.
Separations are not dreams.

Knudsen's Apple-Strawberry juice
lemon yogurt, potato bread toasted
beer, vodka and tonic.
only glasses in the sink.
What are forks for?
The morning's wide bed
empty and my hardon wasted.

Where is the one
who would lie
near me at night
all night?

JULY INVENTORY

7-7 top of the ninth

The hall light is on the bed half empty

Colors - rouge, leaf green, orange day lilies, pink
and green stripes like the shirt the daughter tells
her mother Mark would wear

All the ashtrays full, chips of fallen paint
on the floor

Cooper bloops a single down the leftfield line Doyle
scores from second the Red Sox win "What a crazy
game baseball is!"

Bunker Hill "Where's Boston?" Old Ironsides "The whites
of their eyes"

Ruffian's single tear

Seventeen dollars until next week

Next week the bus to Vermont White River Junction
Montpelier home

A headache at the back of my skull from teaching
from smoking from hunger

One hundred eighty-nine pounds this morning

Olson's *Maximus Three* "I come from the last walking
period of man"

Everyday a shower a shave

Walking in sandals scrapping and flapping
the pavement

Afternoons on the blue couch

A tropical weekend glasses of vodka and tonic sweat

Single grey pubic hair prized

The secret: three thicknesses of newspaper piled
over with grass clippings

Leete's Island Guilford, North Lyme, East Haddam
toy Connecticut towns the entire state like opening
a Whitman's sampler

Mockingbird Morning Dove

Banks of roses dense profusion

One bottletop Two bottletop Three bottletop Four
Don't put your trash in my yard
In my yard

The key? The door?

My right pinky: Heberden's Nodes

                                                    18 July

July's grass burnt over
the gardens are factories.
It is the inexpressible sadness
of a family sitting down to dinner
at a card table under the shade tree
behind their house. This is not enough
and it is not too much.
The screen door slams as the children
go indoors to watch television.
Their parents sit smoking
and talking over the dishes
hardly noticing the buses
rushing past them on the highway.
It is that moment where everything will stay
but never long enough.

28 July

If I abandon poetry
If poetry abandons me
I will be the man who owes
$531 on his gas bill.

3 August

Your hair   the stars
stare up at me
hang above us
longer our short light

4 August

"Can queens be widows?"
Yellow jackets grazing the blackberries
Moths soft and drab at the screen

No one to shave for all by myself
Spent dollars Spent quarters & dimes Spent pennies
Better than bunches clutches of goldenrod
Canoe petals
Cold french fried potatoes though
Hand to mouth a little chin music
Half done intellectual cramps
Scatter rats soon

                                                    5 August

Beverly, I walked down Harvard St.
past the house we lived in
when first married.
The hedges held the rain
while I had dinner with Maggie and Stratis
new friends on this street after ten years.
The house is painted slate gray
it was yellow then
quickly grimed with soot.
The floor to ceiling windows
which sold us on the apartment
dark tonight. Is the bedroom still closet size
with a door to the back porch
the door the man stood in
one night waking us, scaring him away?
On Prospect St. the Finast Market
is a clothing store: the Chinese laundry
where the couple ironed shirts
watching TV, a car insurance store.
You're in Vermont, I'm here
the first time we're leading a double life.
The ten years past
do not sadden me
or seem by memory shortened
packed yes, and the edges obliterated
so that everything fits.
It is the full life in them
I think of walking
these wet, fresh smelling streets
semicircles of dry brick sidewalk
and pavement under the full trees.

Jane - A week ago I woke
with a hangover and the taste of pear
in my mouth. Pear from pear brandy
not so sweet as a comice in autumn
autumn fresh as a child butting in
just as the sun dies here in August
blond on the dead pine branches
or green-gold reflected by the trees
across from me across the colder looking grass
and lake water which means
soon we leave returning to less casual
friendships though not more enduring
or worthwhile or whatever we think
friends are for beyond talking with late at night
when we are restless, as I often am,
and simply don't want to sleep.
But this exuberance is unselfish
like birthdays we all have them
and their celebration is our affirmation
of each other, alive together.

Maybe I like it
the weather "Poet and Pleasant"
today's Boston Globe forecast.

Maybe I like it
the advice "Don't look up - look down"
Edwardians, their newspapers ironed
Shakespeare's word "plumpy", yes, plumpy.

Maybe I like it
resembling the angel
to the left of the Virgin
in Masaccio's Madonna and Child.

Maybe I like it
art as life enhancing

but here in the Northeast Kingdom
the absence of all decoration
all art. What is it?
The weather? The Puritans?
Too much wood?
Too much granite?
Fireplaces, tombstones and foundations.

Maybe I like
beginning a poem in your dream
with the line "Maybe I like it"
A poem about my mother
and not being taken as seriously
as her white or licorice colored dog.
And in the dream
frightened, I bring the poem to you.
You can't understand
my fear. Maybe you like the poem?
But then you recognize
it is not my handwriting
I have no reason to worry.

22 August

What I don't know
no longer makes me talk too much.
The night's sky is a puzzle
full moon behind broken clouds
jigsawed together, soft pieces
colder too and what is the reason
for that or tears over dinner?
The sky puzzle keeps answers
from itself by rearranging
the pieces all of which are
the sky at any one moment.
Is it my plan for paradise
those I love loving one another
at the dinner table one time?
Jenny wakes asking my question:
"Where did everyone go?"

At first the trees are just sick
if leaves are tongues
these licked some bad air
lost their starch red like sores.
Crab apples red "like painted on."
Constant Bliss Moses Sleeper
heavy apple boughs dragging
fall comes this way full.

4-8 September

Don't give me your shot in the thigh look with those
big brown moist cow eyes

The city through clean windows Now clear Now obscure

Hydrangea strawberry shake

Sumac silky red

Asher Benjamin Oreford

Comes down to, to this one day then another

Mice ate the bark now the trees are dying too bright color
among the green firs & yellowing tress in the right light

Your motor's running your fingers drumming

Roadside ferns rusty & maize

Cake like hills

Asters goldenrod mist fills the small valley yellow
slickers in the rain candles up the trail

Another one, fine boned, you press my ankles softly adventurous,
Yes

From the blue couch curved arm
ailanthus spear blade leaves
brick wall in shadow, colder
fading rosy September light graceful
on the regular housetops
east wind ocean clouds above.

12 September

Like removing the cigarette
from between a blind man's lips
before he spits it to the pavement
which the rain lightly stains.
Calmer now soaked to the skin
walking off the morning's dread
heavens open at my feet and the slant rain
makes the sound of gathering
as I long to gather you
in my arms a field of flowers
their fresh and saving gift
pressed to my face some moments.

20 September

Moonshine before morning
the last day of summer.
This afternoon a thief broke open
the front door, had the record player
in our two suitcases when I came in
scaring him off, scaring me.
Over dinner neighborhood gossip
couples in their thirties coming apart
rearranging their lives, lover's vanity
crisp and bracing to them
like the autumn's early apples.

Moonlight floods the kitchen
bright on the stick of butter
color of frost on apples, pears
peaches in the bowl ripening.
The thief escaped, at large
in fear and exhilaration; the lovers
asleep held in their conceit.

23 September

Pardon my wet glove
empty in the outfield
just beyond the skin
or in your hand
spats, barely large enough
to see, attach themselves
to the shucked Oyster shells
grow larger until separated
by someone wearing gloves
using a screwdriver at low tide.

24 September

Cranshaw melon softens
morning garlic breath
sweet pale orange flesh
after green pesto. Waking
my cock stirring
stiffening. Clean sheets.
The rain's lassitude
swampy dream its edge
mists the cooler melon
air. Exotic or obvious
as any hardon's
wayward compass shielded
from the girls. Ouananiche
the land locked salmon
thinking and action one
innocent as the rain

kicks up nitrogen
scenting the summer air
now kicks alley dirt
upon the laundry.

Rain swept from the trees
as leaves to the sidewalk
are arrows pointing
many directions at once.

In the bathtub
soggy wheat having soaked up
the tapwater's impurities
the water let out
a web of body hair
traps kernels at the drain.
Thinner. Absolutely thinner
greater mental awareness
focus on your dictionary word.
Purpose tonight. Tomorrow's assignment
        Nonsense
        Pain
        Existentialism
Love secrets from beyond the grave
ancient diet recipe decoded
Heavenly Blue Seeds, enemas
grass drills, Rocky Mountain poetry
the Mighty Mung thrives
fearfully and wonderfully made
words of God again:
        Linguistics
        Nothing
        Good and Evil
        Pleasure

Old man young
without the comfort
of friends, what?

Nothing is ever over until its done
making it up as I go along

Gray brown froth
goldenrod plumes
at their ruin

Maple & Oak
pale rose leaves
bury themselves.
Enzymes of grass
enzymes of whales
     OMNIA
all things that are lights
love and days
daily new and old.

SPOKEN IN SLEEP

SPOKEN IN SLEEP

For Kenward Elmslie

I

After dinner while the guests are still seated
a woman draws a child's head and clouds
in lipstick on the dining room's picture window.

II

I ask for the 3 bedroom apartment equally
as charming as the one I saw in the right way.
I have blessed this situation with *success*
and passed it on to the Christ within

III

Mother calls. She apologizes. Her mouth's
full of horseshit. The dentist gave it to her:
"After this week . . . will it continue?"

IV

Dear Lewis,
       How are you I got the knife you
sent me. Did you get the pencil I sent you?
I have to study nights now. I get good
marks in all but spelling.
       I have four rabbits and I think I will have
a litter soon. What are you doing this winter
Write soon
              Warren Dill

V

Chocolate pies creamy wedges
chocolate cakes so thick
my throat cracks to say chocolate
fills my mouth like sculpture

VI

Dear Lewis— This is
a picture of our
school here in
the village. Can
you find me? I
will surely send
your little rabbit
next Sat.—Nov. 26—
we will have the
stage leave it at
Campbell's Fruit Store
and it will be there
in the early morning. Be sure
to get him. We sold our
skunk skins for
five dollars. We
have set some
more traps since this
snow melted away. Let
me know how you like
the "Bunny"
                    Warren Dill

VII

Now that dinner's over have a look at these
snapshots. On the one there the leg's like
drool but the Chinese like them of animals.

VIII

I think to myself "It is just the Merritt
Parkway." "Ted Williams was *never*
Governor of Washington!" "There's a fortune in change
here on the ground why doesn't everybody else see it?"

IX

Sowed ice
Went up to the corner
Worked in the Tannary
Worked for Joe Parker Two Days Got Nothing
Split wood
Stormed and blew
Broke roads
Drew wood
Rained stayed at home

Had five dollars in money
Went to see Mable
Got a stiff hat paid $1.50
Walked the street until eleven
Took the midnight train
Jumped off the train
So ended the day

Gathered sap first time
Went with ice first time
Got through at noon

X

Agreeable onions, store cheese, milkweed flowers
frais du bois in a good year, snow peas, shell beans
thumbnail size yellow apples in the grass

XI

My instinct was to reach for his throat
as he stood over me set to attack
and I did but she threw up
toll house cookie batter all over me
then lurched to the open window
where she threw up into the screen

XII

Grasshoppers blacken the oregano
something they spew out
you could use a BB gun at dusk.
You could fix the spider's web
with this kind of metal spray.
Dried blood, cans of urine
or find the woodchuck holes
and fill them with explosives.

XIII

Then in slack times
she puts her hand across her eyes
drums her fingers on her cheek.
She exclaims: "Holy Mud!"

XIV

Jesus Christ cross
roads of our time.
Your premature ejaculator
Alexander Twilight
Service is a *long* word.

XV

A headache something awful
Cloves? Peppermints?

You don't recognize my voice?
You don't know me?
I *know* you!
I don't know Boston lately.

XVI

Ride a cow
Court a bride

Ride a bull
Court a wife

XVII

Unwrapping a double edge razor blade
like it was a stick of chewing gum
the farmer took a life.

XVIII

A grown man softly mumbles
cradling in his arms the tiny
gentleman flopped there whose shocked face
is smooth and yellow in the light.
"Rock-a-bye Baby, Rock-a-by
cleft for thee hite thyself in me"
where the rotten floorboards gave through

XIX

Guinea Keats pullets
small baby Muscovy ducks
Two sows one open one bread
Baby bunnies $1
Child's angora hamster business
to a good home only
Eight full grown
white Embeden geese

Rabbits: three does, one buck
Six monkeys: two Squirrel
one Java, one Cinnamon Ringtail
one large Black Spider
and a Pigtail Macaque
Chickens: Barred rocks and White rocks
Mature Bluetick-Walker male
and trees well

XX

Against the tide my eyes are brown
I didn't know they piled it that high, pardon.
Feeling and thinking are fine
but by the time you get around to them
I'm on the footbridge crossing the Lamoille
my heart is in my mouth.

XXI

Smoking wet hay.
They saved the house
lost the barn, are burning
what's left of the barn
making ends meet.

XXII

All the green world
over mist is rising
like in a Chinese painting
ascending from the valleys
to the hills curling there.
The sky rolls down
its sooty colored fields
ripped every so often
a blue lake peers through
and rain loose as ashes.
This shed of rain
we've been inside
looking out all week
time to get out from under.

XXIII

Urban is a pitcher's name
and Dizzy, Dutch, Rube and Babe.
Henry and his brother Christy
Mathewson won more games
than any other brothers ever
until the Perry's Gaylord and Jim.
"Poets think they are pitchers
but they're really catchers"—Moe Berg
who could speak seven languages
and not hit a curveball in any of them.

Babe Ruth spoke to me later

XXIV

He came right up to me
bold as brass this salesgirl
with a smartaleck puss on
"Where so proudly we hail
as the twilight fast gleaming"
Some day you'll have the shakes
you'll weigh three hundred pounds
your children will be little bastards
you won't have a hair on your head
then you'll know you'll know even then
that all through your lifetime . . .
Prayers! Prayers, concluded the boy defective.
Why can't I get the room
to stop turning and mind me?
Goodnight Irene I'll see you
in my dreams
                    Sincerly,
                              Bunny Rabbit

XXV

Son, here's a swimming pool
a dog that will take your arm off
and beat you over the head with it

and a paper asshole.
Here son, take my horse and gun
in short, the tools of ignorance.

XXVI

Mustard, custard and you
you big shit But baby
my heart must weigh about a pound.
These are the recollections of olden days:
    "We used no mattress on our hands
    No cage upon our face;
    We stood right up and caught the ball
    With courage and with grace."

XXVII

The burning drunks their fiery deaths.
I am a detective with evidence on my hands
cringing from a shot right in the face.

XXVIII

Take me out of the ballgame
Take back your peanuts and cracker jacks!
Those thoroughly delicious morsels available throughout
the country albeit occasionally in the tougher
neighborhoods for some unexplainable reason.
I don't care if I never come back!

XXIX

The same wind that in May carried
blossoms to the ground now brings apples
klunking down. Apple knockers pale green appleness.

XXX

Mr. Stratton who wore a vest
but could not find it trapped a crow
because the crows would not mind him.
After he plucked the feathers from one wing
Stratton painted the crow's flesh barn red
to warn other crows from his garden.

ESKER

Candles high in leafy chestnut mansions
old brick rolling sidewalks . . .
                    "A single shape
is made magnificent by perennial touching."

THE HAIRENIK ASSOCIATION, INC. 1939

Thirties rounded letters carved in sandstone
what sensations of revulsion
                    "Delicate hairs in the broth
                    of my corned beef and cabbage
                    Waiter, I'll need a comb for this!"
emanate from this beige stone facade
drifting awkwardness, shame past humiliation
(No one ever enters or leaves)
dedicated to the proposition
that humans have created an inhuman world

POST INDUSTRIAL MAN   En203
A survey of the novel focusing upon the gradual
corruption of sensibilities and the increasing
degradation and vulgarization of values from
Smollett to Beckett   (3 credits)

I wrote an autobiography
What did I write about?
"the red-breast entertains us with his autumnal song"
Coy and prudish wheedling
                    "I daresn't have any
                    before dinner," I'd say
Our Bill with a nice firm little ass
to hold his pants up
                    Thunderclaps
rain like gravel.
Chinese lanterns from the rafters
burnt and melted telephone, lithograph
of a mule staring right at you
octagonal lampshade faraway room.

Six days slate grey and green
like a steel engraving the piney crags
black coast of Albania we've raised
or charred Dresden dim ferocity
the blank polished sandstone meekly gleams
I am of that farthest come behind
                              cruder weapons dusty
bland sunlight through venetian blinds stirs
                         as if I were a free man

KAME

Morning letter haze
                    you were talking in the dream
                    wake pen in hand, aubade
                                        yellow legal pad
Loves me Loves me not Never
loved me if she loves me not as much

                    where we were has a new address

Darkness is coming to our people here in Oakland
                    this once blue shirt dimming purple tears
                    when you put it on

There's no chance
                    we'll go for the festival of the chariots
                                        chanting tasting prasdas
                                        MERCY
                                        AUSTERITY
                                        TRUTHFULNESS
                                        CLEANLINESS
& other of the swami's youthful pastimes

I don't want to repeat anything
                    that I'm not saying to someone
                    to fix anything by routine
                    furthers everyone's expectations
                    needlessly

the fly avoids my fingers

                    like smoke struggling from the farmer's mouth
                        walking his fields
blue chickory   queen anne's lace   loosestrife   asters
this fall I will regain the room
                        above the streets
whose light promises contemplation and rest

An old man shakes his heart from his shirt pocket
rain clacks on the roof Thetford Hill late early now
                    "I'm turning into a bowl of mush. Young
                    people should try everything until they

find what they can do but you could
take pictures of your mother naked
making chicken soup."

ANY MAN WHO HAS A MOTHER OUGHT
TO REVERE ALL WOMEN IN HER NAME

You were never the sort of person to say: "But we don't
ask you to leave when you come to our house at breakfast time."
This kind of person pauses to say as you're piling slash:
"You're not going to burn the woods down are you?"

Today my head's on the fritz after last night
making letters slowly
     I don't want to be drunk
    wearing out my personality
        spotted and imperfect
    don't want to be bored either
Press your face into these just pulled from the earth carrots
    Refreshed? Disciplined?

     There were stars clearly there earlier
     come again through the veil sweet
     hindrance what hurries crisp light
     at the fringe
        heaven's dew upon the earth

DRUMLIN

Poised, alert, slightly distant, severe like Wittgenstein

    in photographs   But in life?

Around the eyes the message

        that you can be hurt

crushed, calf's eyes

        who wept stars? Who saw to weep?

The moon the letter C backwards

```
C I R C L E
I C A R U S
R A R E S T
C R E A T E
L U S T R E
E S T E E M
```

This is the '70's

    a decade even Elvis Presley's death

        cannot redeem

they say   a hole in time   blank pages

suppose all our writing over them

        is no improvement?

The man who reads auras did he see

        a squared halo

above Groucho's dome

                a raspberry upon his lips

                      for Mrs. Calabash

                            everywhere she is?

            The horse takes the cake

            The horse eats the cake

            Hi ho the tablecloth too

After the krazy hat competition

            they heard a bestiary

                      and barn danced

cleaned their rooms   disciplined their children

wiped their hands and feet

were fun to work beside felling trees to save

the family place from wrack and ruin

           "Watch what you're dragging in.

           I *never* show it when I'm

           depressed. Never. Why does he

           have a hair up his ass anyway?"

Covered in feathers under her wing.

Rain from a trough

                        fits of paper tearing

fallen green crescent pine cones sticky underfoot

        the green turns yellow
        under the clear blue sky
        crickets sing at noon downed
        apples rotting sweet scent
        overhead blue doors & depths
        soon must leave for good

MONTPELIER BISCUIT

Black   Red   Brown   Grey   White

nightroads barn   leafless trees   sky, rock, ice   snow

Not everyone knows what it's like

                   Green- Pine, spruce

as once a concussion

         crumpled star points

17th cold cold cold 18th

       19th A to Z to Snooze

```
┌─────────────────────────┐
│      T U E S D A Y       │
│                         │
│          2 0            │
│                         │
│   Around the John Hancock│
└─────────────────────────┘
```

people walk cheerlessly

the wind yanks at your

hat you slap it back

upon your head too hard

rattling your brains

cursing

        snow wet smacks

R E M E M B E R

DEATH

21st   popcorn   cranberries   ribbon candy

streets like black rubber scuff marks

old brick city thickest of reds

upright they are soldiers

sailors when they slant

perched at land's end

22nd   Not one bird but berries

bunches in garden trees

23rd   Bell   Star   Circle   cookies

It's the softness of things

themselves giving the feeling

they are about to transform

themselves into indeterminate

shapes one will not

wish to hold but nudge

24th Eve

I'm not here because

I want to be here

I don't want to be

anywhere else

Uncertainty?   Bananas

Yarn God's eye   red & blue tin elephant

purple plastic star burst   angels of wood shavings

the folds of their garments

bouquets of peaches

& green sprigs in their arms

one figure walking the sidewalk

his scarf his breath

what speech is this

ghostly form disintegrating

chewed at the edge like stamps

leaky boots

you won't find the answer

in a letter lost for now

Christmas

A sleigh's wooshing hush

running fresh

jolly comice pear wobbles

on the table   white bells

let nothing you dismay

Hunched shoulders hands stuffed in jacket pockets

gray like the 40's

but like a welcome crease

when life was simpler

everyone relaxed from war

dreams laid to rest

who mourns in lowly exile here?

HENRIETTA MENCH

It's rain, it's warm
for New Year's Eve.
Grandmother, she bathed
my chest, bandaged my cuts
carried me up the stairs
washed vomit and mud
from my face, told me
not to go out so
sloppy at the neck—
she meant a tie. She died
last night weighing seventy
pounds on an oscillating
bed. I walked to
Wing Wings in Chinatown
past the Greek grocer's
round New Year's bread
and bought bok choy
water chestnuts, bitter
melon thinking rain might
turn to snow. She often
recalled playing with Edna
Small among cemetery stones
when snow shut Wilkes Barre
schools in 1897 or '98.
She liked waffles with
chicken gravy or a little
sauerkraut and pork.

ALISON'S LETTER
USED AS A BOOKMARK
FOR UNGARETTI'S POEMS

That the death of a child
your sister whose leg broken
lies in hospital, my own daughters
is the vision we cannot face
a horror to derange us so
we make a noise never heard
before, I don't know but
is to imagine this death not
a sign that there is something
worse beyond what our mind
will allow into which we
must be led before we go?
Arden nearly died (she loves
to hear the story, her own miracle)
of spinal meningitis she was
not two. I beat my hands
against the floor, choked to
cry and when she did not die
I scared myself that she
might or Marni in some
accident, one vicious sudden
flight, be ripped from me.
This need to poison myself
with such fearful imagining
steal my breath, prepare
my nerves to obey what?
There is the scar on
Arden's foot where hospital
IV fed her. She lay there
we were helpless to stay
or go in dread that she
might sigh and leave alone.
Opening the window
Ungaretti scattered crumbs
to lure the shrill sparrows
a distraction for his
nine year old dying son.

A TORN PAGE

What abuse
will not foreshorten
curtail my life
will stall but
like a fence
will keep me walking
up and down
making up in my head
speeches
  for voice is the root
and my heart sees
weighed what my lips
speak.
  Wisdom stays from my door.
Then in silence
the cold lump self
still & sullen
inhardened the others
distant or near lost
  what's on woodwork
baseboard, moulding the scratches
what shines circled
in dimness what calls
without shape
  but from inside
that Sunday afternoon
as quiet as the snow
falling that quietly
I worked polishing
my shoes when the gray
outside calmed me
so in a single lustre
the snow at the window
me, shoe in hand
reflecting the desk lamp
  earnestly reaching
  earnestly grasp
looking up my head clear
the whole inside a pearl

Marie's irises
what with the furnace
out overnight the whites
unfurled slowly
            Spring now
here not just yet
but robins on the feeble
green dirty winter strewn grass
squirrels yes and pigeons
sheets on the line
            crisp March
crocus breaking through
the low sun blinding
smeared and dusty window
tongues of egg yellow
these purply blue and
white arching flowers
on tall stalks
            like torches

RUNAWAY POND: A SHORT VERSION

For
Bernadette Mayer
Jay Boggis
Jane Gunther

Lilac more grape than lavender
crowds, taps the window here
Sheffield Heights second spring.
This purple I want to crush
against my lips gather dandelion
yolks from the field hundreds
of sunny heads, bees cover them.
In Boston lilac perfume filled
the room the evening it was May
and the next summer. Two 95
degree days like a trick
lengthened Boylston Street. Spring
too came overnight, and you could
not see across the Public Garden
by morning. Horse chestnut seeds
like creme horns and drifting
where they fell in gutters
or stamped in alley mud the fallen
seeds tiny white wafers bear
a crimson mark. Wisteria hung glamorously
from an alley fence the smell rising.

Ailanthus barbaric crowns erupt last
like tufts sit at the end of branches.
When the month began all leaves were
puckered like wings now there are clouds
over the Garden orange, chartreuse—un-
natural like cheap clothing—old ivory
and coppery green where the great beeches
spread, leaves profligate in their energy
grow from the tree trunks. Soft dogwood
petals in the grass. The magnolia burst
pink and white then gone nearly the middle
of May, birthdate of three friends.

I spent the spring walking around Boston
agitated, talking to myself sometimes out loud
arguing with people in my head I no longer
spoke to or had said it all I thought.
Pestered like the couple in their sixties
picketing city hall for over thirteen years
they carry hand-lettered signs something
about their house broken into and a
nephew who died in VIET NAM. Ignatius Foley
whose head tilts to the left, whose chin
sits on his chest walks near the couple
wearing a sandwich board "ABORTION IS MURDER"
and has done so for years. I walked with
these people or thought I did when passersby
stare as I vehemently speak, compelled
by some inner switch to bitch and argue
out loud gesturing as I walk.

"Wild, startled and distrustful" like
the red-haired woman. I saw her stand
and scream "SON OF A BITCH" stunned
by her reflection in a store window
"Yooouuu SONOFABITCH you!"
She stopped me as I walked down
Newbury Street thrust her finger
at my neck and shrieked "Jesus Saves
yes Jesus Saves but not you
you Mother FUCKER!"

There is an English poet
on the Common who stops students
asking for a small loan until
his inheritance comes through
Thursday or Friday.
'Yankee Doodle Dandy' subway whistler
Warlock Noel, Witch Leslie. The blue suited
man clipping away all day at the morning papers.
I keep mumbling cursing and my throat
gripped by rage . . . These lines
    "And I will no more write
    of the bloody bearded woman
    who rose dripping from me
    Goddamn her Goddamn me
    Amend . . ."

I sought to marry with Captain Video's
death, make a poem for Donald Haberman
that he might leave my dreams re-enter
my life. Got no further. "For how long
does it take crudities to become beauties?"
Continued to record my dreams until they too
were pushed aside or simply kept to themselves
after the one about not arguing with people
you are arguing with in life.
When the air sweetened I slept like a baby
sweet air's caress, ardent for sleep
blessed afternoons on the blue couch
waking without voices in my head.
Read something, woke and wrote:
"There is another world and it is here too."
Fallen in upon myself, hibernating
damp, mean cave and snaggle-toothed when
I come out. Wearing out the fever
not conquering, short of operating
on myself like the twenty year old
who first removed his testes then opened
himself up after his adrenal gland
to quiet his sexual and aggressive feelings.
The pain his liver gave him as he worked
to push past it cut him short.
Chester Morris, on shipboard, kept going
with a kitchen knife and whisky
guiding his hands in an overhead mirror
and came up with his appendix despite
the typhoon. After twenty-eight years
the American G.I. left the single room
in which he hid, did not want to leave
had failed at suicide and so
turned himself in. His protector, she
was dead of cancer, had come from her
deathbed to see him before she died
making her "very happy" he was certain.
Same morning I found thirty-two dollars
in a white envelope in the street
blank envelope except for the pencil
notation "8 Marks." That makes thirty-five
dollars and countless pennies found this year
keeping my eyes to the ground.
Kierkegaard says anxiety is

"The dizziness of freedom." No!
The dizziness of breaking free.

The eight banty hens are not the company
Rob said they might be, but the fire
is conversation, I'm not lonely being alone
first time in five years. Red-winged blackbird
swaying at the slim top of a chokecherry bush.
Two eggs so far, the first blood-streaked.
Swallows come and go in the barn easily spooked
magenta backs, buff breasts and throats
the color of orange sunsets. A gray
squirrel thinks he owns the place at night,
has excavated two Yellow Delicious apples
fastidiously leaving the skin scattered
curled up like brown wrapping paper.
This morning I saw the butter
was gnawed and kept coming across
his tiny avocado colored turds
on the windowsill and kitchen counter.
He woke me when he knocked over
some spice tins. Some nerve. South
wind. Rain softly boiling, gurgle
on the roof. Mist leaving
the field obscuring the trees.
Scratch black fly bites wrists
and hairline. Lumps with red dots.
Soft city hands garden work
blisters and sore a scab
forming on the side of my thumb.
Burrow my head in the pillows. Sleep.

Less spring and summer diminished surely
radio off no noise of baseball
Martin and Woods gone and in their places
thin, unstoried voices "Sincere" Ken Coleman
"Eager Beaver" Rico Petrocelli who as a player
prepared for one season at shortstop
by playing the drums all winter.
They speak and the game jerks along
into shallow right, rounds first, hustles back
and I've lost track, can't see it.
The nearest Globe is seven miles
I'm unable to follow Peter Gammons

he of the fresh simile each time
Rice homers. After leaving Fenway one shot
"registered for the New Hampshire primary."
Levi Cole has smoked no bacon
but as he butchers he wears his Red Sox cap.
The Hardwick bars are closed
("electronic gambling devices")
boarded over. Rough shit kicker
"Woodchuck" bars empty they add
their weight to Hardwick's already
bowed down air. The two-year-old
double murder remains unsolved
but anyone in Hardwick will tell you
the police know who it is, are handcuffed
because the killer is the lunatic son
of one of the town's prominent families
"He'll never be arrested" they shake
their heads side to side wisely.
In Glover the taxidermist has moved
a work table to face the picture window
replacing the tableau of bear cubs
who sat fishing from rowboats smoking
corncob pipes as trout swam in the
plastic water where the boats floated.
The taxidermist's son makes fur coats
and ridiculous skunk hats it's a wonder
anyone would be caught dead in. His father
put a mole on a slab of plastic grass,
had a fish covered in leopard fur
and stuffed a farmer's two headed calf.
He could have done the polar bear
let loose by vandals in Pawtucket, R.I.
and shot by a posse of seventy
to save the residents of a trailer park.
Seventy guns blazing!
Any in that posse might have been among
the one hundred volunteers interviewed in Florida
from which twelve witnesses were chosen
to be present at Spenkelink's death.
"I wondered if he was dead. I saw
the smoke rising from his leg
and knew it was over." So reported
destiny's correspondent Thomas H. Slaughter.
"String 'em up by their balls like they

did in Florida" agrees the Barton grocer
with his friend a future volunteer
you bet! to watch two Burlington bank robbers
get what's coming to them. I didn't say a thing
haven't said a word in two days
other than "It might" in reply to
a question about all the rain
we've been having. Eight months silent
Gary Crawford of St. Albans his voice
cracked as he spoke over the radio
"Every living thing is the living speck of eternity."
Gary works for a newspaper, on Thursdays
will resume his silence for sure quitting
again for good after the fall solstice.
He's putting together a book
of all the written messages he used
and saved while he was silent.
A week ago at this hour I was teaching
talking, now there are only three hens
hiding under a bush to scare or
sweet talk back into their coop
they flew out of in this afternoon's
hellacious thunderstorm.

My Irish fisherman's sweater!
My poet's sweater! Dylan Thomas
Sean Connery sweater! Gone!
Left at Mattie's Sewing Shop
since before Christmas
remember just this minute she closed
for good on Memorial Day.
Mattie was in the South End
when we came ten years ago.
We almost bought the house of a crazed
disabled W.W. II veteran but the man
selling it didn't own it then we found ours
vacant without plumbing the copper pipe
boosted no kitchen thick coats
of blue green (color of cooked
canned peas), brown cheap paint.
We couldn't afford the house today
couldn't even afford rent in the new
apartments remodeled from old houses
where the new "gentry" lives.

We are gentry too being palefaces
we qualify and we are responsible
for "gentrification" meaning fewer Puerto Ricans
and poor blacks and no low-income housing.
Finishing touches like digging up the streets
to lay new sewer pipes big enough
kids walk through them upright.
Then brick sidewalks and young trees.
Ten years ago across the alley from us
a gray-bearded black lady ran a wino flophouse
and the alley had cats, spraying Toms
slowly strolled ruling the alley fences
bulging muscle, or so it looked, hunched
at their necks. Scars, we were told,
from many battles. They're gone.

25 May
    Cloudy
Lena came up I
went back with her
She is making a white coat
26 May
    Rained
Mended & planted
dahlias. Order
came from S&R co.
27 May
    Rained all day
Dot B. Came up to
dinner. Went up to
Vence school in pm
28 May
    Cloudy
Went down home
Came home with Maurice
And so nameless wrote in her diary every day
of 1932, wrote something on the four
narrow lines in pen or pencil. Her diary
fits into the palm of my hand.
Glenwood, the stove's name.
The wood stove is a P.D. Beckwith
"Round Oak." Susan Smith Age 10
February 10th some 19th-century year
finished sewing the "Do Unto Others" sampler.

Yesterday at this hour I heard
the squirrel in the ceiling overhead.
I was standing by the stove still
as a post when he crawled *down*
the wall to the floor and crouching
he half hopped across the floor
leapt up on a chair and from there
the table when he picked up a plum tomato
carried it to the edge of the table
took a snapping bite and cast it aside
to disappear under the table for a second
reappearing with a chestnut.
He brought this to his mouth
as if it were a communion wafer
and in several sharp, flicking nibbles
he had the shell off and was gnawing
at the meat when I somehow moved
and he took off up the wall skittering
across the ceiling nut in mouth.
Dinner time. Bourbon or Vodka?
Grape lilac against gray sky.
Mock orange branches or stalks
in the window like Joe's grass boxes.
Winter's dead house flies very light
crumbly caught in cobwebs. Miss Marni
Arden, Beverly. Their day's incidents
and events. Talk at the table.
Set my place by kerosene lamp
and quickly finished frying pan
and mustard cooking. A cigar
by the geranium on the front porch
you can hear cars and an occasional
whooshing trailer truck across the valley
on the interstate, inter-country
bound for Montreal or New York
heartening to the ears of a city boy.
What was it Harrison used to say?
"Think of Michigan as a mitten." I am
warm my hand stopping to piss
on a large floppy burdock leaf
now glistening then steams.
Bird song, nameless birds, joyous
swallows swoop past the apple tree's
few pink blossoms and a great crow's

belligerent, nagging cry farther off
over pine and spruce at the edge
of the meadow. Soft gray above
and beyond. No hills today. Alone.
Gray hairs here and there in my
beard. Deep dorylike tub. A moment's
evening sunlight lights the floor.
Single dark hair thin crescent
on Ivory soap cake.

Less than postcard size photo
of Jon's painting. the flour white
boy and his family, is what I brought
tacked to the lathe to look at
if I lift my eyes from the reflection
of my unshaven, double-chinned face
in the silver slip-on tea cozy.
At noon the bell tones
Liberty Lobby's Jew-baiting spokesman
comes from the radio giving who
knows who the news about
"Bellicose Begin" and the gas crisis
brought home where it belongs
to Israel's door. "Who is Carter for
anyway?" and this is Lyndonville's
college rock 'n' roll station
playing "Alice's Restaurant" every day!
I wonder if Levi and Oona
listen as they break for lunch
from their butchering or Lewis
come in from work in the nursery.
He planted horseradish "for our Jewish
friends" new settlers carried north
in the Hippie migration. The first Jew in
his town came fifty years ago
to walk his tuberculosis off
around Caspian Lake. Jon's grandfather
Naphtali Herz Imber King of Jewish
Bohemia in America wrote, words
or music I forget, the Israeli
national anthem. "Is this," the
commentator's voice is lowdown pleading,
"any way to run a government?"

As if rolled in flour the boy
powerfully built like a fireplug
tough looking rascal has he seen
something that his father's
hand around his upper arm means
to keep him from? The mother clings
to this father who has his arm
around his red haired daughter
and alone looks straight ahead.
It could be something the others,
the women, fear that the father is
ignoring thus maintaining his courage
and humiliating them. Something
that will cause his clown white
son to hurtle toward it into
more than mischief. This boy
who is a thug or prince or
he is just poised earlier
than most to break away. I don't know
if I was about to cut myself free
when my father did it for me.
He fled his wife and family
friends and patients, changed his life.
(How many times will I be
compelled to write this?)
I was cheated. Betrayal weakened me
but I was cheated. Unlike the boy
lacking his thrusting physical charge
I was restless, squirming, burdened
to get out from under, become abstract
like my father, exist only in the act.

Crawly bugs through the forest
on my legs. A long nosed one
up on all six quivering filaments
drills for blood, takes too long, dies.
That cowbird seems to sit in air
the wire invisible against the dark
hillside hemlocks. Why doesn't the
bird get zapped if that's electric line
or jolted by a phonecall? Even the
man who gets the wrong number says
"Thank you much." Mustard and buttercup
take over from May's field yellowing

dandelions all that's left
are grizzled frothy heads.
You can hear rain coming in distant
booms and in the maple tree's
and bottom's up birch leaves. Clouds
darken overhead. The lilac is a day
or so past its peak lavender cones
dimming color of raspberry ripple
yogurt. That was breakfast. The ant
in all his armor or like a pre-
W.W. II sedan knows the way
over my green toed (grass cutting)
sneaker. To have bitched and pouted
and ultimately often cried over
mowing the front lawn all my young
life! Getting eaten alive.

     June 6th remembered on the granite
     scroll carved on a granite memorial block
     as the day Runaway Pond got its name.
"Previous to this strange occurrence the body of water was called
Long Pond, and its outlet normally ran south. The residents of
Glover wished to divert the water into a northern outlet, so it
would flow down into Mud Pond, raising the water level there and
furnishing more power for the mills along the Barton river. Long
Pond was 150 feet above the level of Mud Pond, with a very sharp
drop between the two. On June 6, 1810, about 60 men assembled
to celebrate 'June Training Day' by cutting a channel to form a
northern outlet from Long Pond into the other body of water.
The barrier holding the north end of Long Pond was a solid bar
that resembled frozen gravel, through which they proceeded to
cut. Unknown to workers there was a species of quicksand deposit
underneath the·bar of hardpan, and once the bar was pierced this
sand started washing away rapidly, undermining the whole north
shore of the pond. Alarmed at the sudden great rush of water, the
workmen scrambled to the safety of higher lands. Riders pounded
down the valley warning settlers to flee from the path of the
torrent. Eyewitnesses declared that the earth trembled and shook
as the water broke loose with a tremendous deafening roar. At
the start there was a rush of water toward the center and the
whole pond boiled like a cauldron. Two loons caught on the sur-
face were unable to rise from the water, so great was the suction.
The great wall of unleashed water tore a path 30 to 40 rods wide
and 30 to 60 feet deep, demolishing gristmills, uprooting large

trees and boulders, carrying everything before it. Long Pond was emptied of water in one hour and fifteen minutes. After the water had drained out, mud ran for several hours. In six hours the flood surged into Lake Memphremagog at Newport, a distance of more then twenty miles."

> Summer of 1811 coltsfoot flowered
> in the thousands sprang where the water
> had left a path of mud and
> balm of Gilead appeared
> for the first time hereabouts
> more sign for the people of Glover,
> Barton doubtless all around to ponder
> while they sought a way
> to read the water's headlong flight,
> ransom what their greed had made.

The wild day from the north
wind that thrashes what's left
of the lilac flowers to the grass
in the north is bluegray pushing
rain squalls soon but overhead
smart blue holes and sunlight's
breakthrough on the near ridge moving
shadow on the far ridge all at once.
Heat film over the wood stove
like witch water. There is the snake
skin I found and pinned to the wall
lifting like a banner in the draft.
Mother has reached the age
when her friends die. Joe, the man
who raised goats for milk who told
a joke about in college having "a cute
way of getting on and off."
They will all be gone before
too long who were the adults
in my life and none will replace
them, none can but ourselves in the
eyes of our children yet we demand
of each other that we be different.
And we are, but who as a child
recognizes this when they are all
so much bigger and smarter.
John Wayne died today. He will
not be replaced but he will be called

for like Patty Hearst's mother
wanting to know where all the real
men, all the Clark Gables have
gone. My Hungarian grandmother died
last June. To her eldest son she left
ten dollars. Cheap insurance to
guarantee immortality through at least
her grandchildren's generation.
There are families, men and women,
in whom such selfishness and cruelty
abounds, becomes hideous, lashes them
and self-pity in excess coldly
derides others, denies their love!
We escape from these our need is great
into other families casting baggage aside
we think

Common fleabane faded nightgown pink
Indian paintbrush Assyrian curls
Crown vetch blown from the highway's banks
Bunchberry related to dogwood
though close to the ground
The bedsheet white cream and pink lipped
peony soft hammer leaning over
But read Guy Davenport without a dictionary!
And no library in Glover
Barton nearest open only some afternoons
where find shindy, gaster, bdellium, rimple
words in the mind's grasp shaggy then buttered
silken finishes gruff?
            What he knows makes a noise
like chomping celery and prints
itself cleanly like a hoof.
I know beavers are vegetarians
but like better Joe's explanation
that with their tails they stun
fish then turn to eat them.
Bears go up to 400 pounds around
here. Milk is sold in pounds. Forty
pounds a day from each of Gaylin's cows.
The state's moose census stands at
50 to 100 in the "Big Woods."
Names will do, will not daisy game
apricots not fruit

                on my morning cereal
sink your teeth into
dandelion then paintbursh now white clover
what might flowers stand for?
No appetite for lamb patties
I want "Wooly Burgers!"
served up by Ernie the singing butcher.
"Genius is time?"
Well, patience my virture
and anger, hair trigger, my cross
and talking too much and . . .
Civilization, did you write, is light
tell the time by the sun's
nearly rhomboid print on the floor
climbing the walls to a line.
Pipkin, sovereign (the coin) words
Marni and Arden want
and Canaan but does that mean
where it is?
Because I want to know where
knowing Latrobe's glass lined tanks
are across the state from dread
Three Mile Island and Maureen Owen
can lift a bottle with me!
"The fate to become a thing may not be so
terrible as the pressure to become a seer."
Fairfield Porter wrote that and wasn't it
Pound who said something like if
you back an American into a corner
he comes out with a quote.

Holding the poetry tabloid against the wind
folding it with difficulty, my mind strays
from the large photographs of the poets
set above their poem or two like macro-
cephalic heads atop the puny body
of their work like the Shadow Lake
camper who has named his camp Lynga On.
My favorite poets right this minute
are Whalen, Schuyler, and Edward Thomas, bachelors
I hope never to see their pictures here.
But Allen Ginsberg is on the cover
smiling in a pin-striped suit and why not
applause for those who are sensitive too?

His poems are all about the things
he must do that serve to keep him
from writing poems. In Vermont I read
everything. Well, I read what will
distract me or what I can be distracted
from with no loss and like a voice-over
I can think over as I read
sports magazines, detective stories
any magazine including *Gourmet*,
this book of interviews with writers
Ginsberg among them not the Whitman
or Milton I brought hoping to get serious,
settle down with them again and steal
some of that thunder instead hope-
lessly addicted to eye candy: leave
Milton, Whitman to winter when my eyes
can't be brought up by the gliding
red-winged blackbird's stop in air
and lands on the tree branch sways.
Orange wing. It is nearer orange above
the yellow chevron. I get back to these
pages before I lose it, but the book
slides from my lap to the grass. Star trivet.
A passage on the ferns the way
they curve out so openhandedly
greener and casting green into the light
of the wood's shade. Which ferns did
Jay pick and offer me the roots
"Here, try some Maine bananas."
Or something unpleasant for instance
those Barton storekeepers
who refuse Canadian coins
but with Yankee cunning
give them in change. I want
to roll out of bed and get it on paper
before the water has boiled, the hours
pass and my arthritic hands clench.

The newspaper photograph of my white-bearded
father taken March 19, 1975 in Ontario, California is the first
time I have "seen" him in fourteen years. He stands woodenly,
this veteran of many small town newspaper photographs, hands in
pants pockets, posed as if talking to the doctor across from him
in front of a family health clinic my father will head. "The medi-

cal staff is headed by Dr. William T. Corbett, a general practice physician, who speaks several languages." The clipping reached me through the daughter I have never met of the only uncle I have but have not seen in nearly thirty years. She came across the photograph on vacation, sent it to her father who gave it to my mother who sent it to me

arriving on this day
there are schools of cottony clouds
reaching down the valley and
everywhere overtop and distant
to where the sky is pale blue.
The farthest hills beyond Lyndonville
like veils I want to say but what
would they be suspended from or hold them up?
Flimsy anyway or like clothing
casually tossed that is the impression
a backdrop for all the valley's
pocket landscapes, one housetop, the road
rises up to hold your eyes two yellow
lines organize the hollows and
hills curve together. The sparkle
of a tin rooftop. Rusted barn roof.
A frost this late in June forecast
for this valley tonight. My father
had ten years to learn
"several languages." He knew
Hungarian, some Italian and
bedside Polish I think when he left
and the note on his office door read:
"I have gone to further my education."

The match to the gas, tiny jets
dancing alone, bacon jiggles
three putty-blue small eggs
dancing I will, alone
I will shake the peony flowers
no one gives a damn
shake the kerosene lamp
I don't wipe my feet
across my mouth
I don't go with those who do
I live with a family of squirrels
who eat from a compost bucket
White-blonde girl red-tailed

blue bird tattooed above her breast
hot ticket local talent
Hezzie Somers's strawberries
"not one to know about my ancestors"
                    Hezzie sez
sugar jam pink drops stuck
that's my song
                    "And named the baby rock 'n' roll"
Dancing I do shuffle and thump
the floor barefoot, naked
dripping from the tub

A city of lightning bugs in the field

Morning cobwebs across eyes
and ankles bumping into doorframes.
Last evening a rainbow stub
in the southeast corner.
Pasture under cloud roof
the pearl curtain lifts
smoky edges soft dome
the pasture is a pilgrim's
cloak flung wide behind
running north and the devil's apron
shaking out stones like crumbs
and a bird veering in flight
an angel nothing that is not itself
one foot up the stairs.
To be slow to be whole.

FEBRUARY 29TH

The deepfreeze. Fourteen degrees. Ducks
are off the pond's scant open water
and on the Garden's macadam walks
and matted brown grass. The only green
the male mallard's hood and neck—
Japanese beetle blue-green. When
the sun hits it the color stings.
This kind of cold bright—a metallic
taste in the mouth—day coming
in from the outdoors with a thirst
brought on by the raw air a cold beer
tastes great. "Fix me one of those,
my mouth's awful dry." That's what
grandmother wanted often summer nights
watching a hand on TV fill a pearled glass
with Schmitt's or Miller's. I did.
She drank, made a face and passed
the glass to me. "Here you finish
this. Why is it they never taste
as good as they look?" Skaters, even
the clumsy forward leaning ones,
the hockey players and those bent
ankled Norman Rockwell models, when you
look from them wobbling, falling or
suavely turning over the Duck Pond ice
to red brick Beacon Street and
east to the giants of downtown's
financial district (huge theatrical
clouds of electric plant steam behind)
or to the buff lower stories of the Ritz
and above to naked tree branches (How
like Franz Kline's signature!) and
their dent on an airmail paper blue sky
you get, I do, the sensation of being
in two places at once. Pope John Paul's
October visit left the lower Common trampled
into mud set now like detective's plaster
around frozen footprints. Days before
the Pope's mission a Black teenage
football player was gunned down
huddling in a Charlestown field

waiting for the next play to run
hundreds of yards from two boys
pulling a trigger and paralyzed
by their bullet Darryl, the boy,
lies still in a hospital bed.
In shame many of his fellow Bostonians
signed a covenant and wear a pin
signalling their call for an end to racial
violence pronounced "Rachel" so many
times each day some may think violence
has been named like a hurricane: a tomato
soup red pin on which a branch sprouts leaves
of white, olive drab (Who is this color?)
brown, black, yellow: a pin as ugly
as homemade sin making plain that right
thinking can only be corrupted by good
looks. Down Charles Street lived Cynthia
in a top floor apartment all pitched
ceilings and queer angles. She wrote,
a novelist, addicted to Jung and, I came
to think, a Jewish American Princess
who "went to the mountain" knowing she
was dying of cancer and died there.
The "mountain" being in New Mexico and
her not quite forty or just forty having
spent most of her working life writing
one novel obsessed by insects. A book
I read and liked and remember her joy
in hearing praise. One night over dinner
we agreed to keep dream journals
for three months then compare what we
dreamt with the idea that some wave-
length might connect us dreaming at
night. I took her journal and arranged
the prose into several poems, and sent
these to her thoughtlessly if that can
be said to mean never imagining things
could turn out as they did. "How dare you,"
Cynthia replied, "Those are *my* words
not yours. Don't ever think for a minute
of ever publishing that stuff." After this
we saw each other but twice in Vermont,
far northern Vermont, where she had a house
had gone on my say so that it was hardly

123

ever hot in Vermont and then not for long
only to arrive during the hottest summer
in anyone's memory. You expect someone
you know, a contemporary, to die either
violently or otherwise before their time
and mourning them the world unsheathed
cuts deep, lays open flesh so you
shudder, stretch, yawn . . . the shudder
shakes you like a hand in dread and
relief. Who will, wonders a voice
in my head, be next and where will I
hear of it? Vermont? Like Gordon and
Donald? How black the thought, silky voice
and glad not to be overheard but feel
the guilty pleasure of . . . of what? Listening
to the sweet poisonous dark voice at all?
What poison? Not being good? Making speeches
over the grave in tears and glory writing
obituaries in my head . . . it passes. From here
across Charles Street the skaters stride
noiselessly stopping and starting their
skates throwing up spray. Does the ice melt
disappearing one March night into air or
vanish below the water and disappear
there? The state house prepares with flags
and an electronic voice counting off one . . .
two . . . three for Eruzione, Silk, McClanahan
and sleepy handsome Jim Craig who here
in triumph come today. They *were* something!
They *are* rousing where Carter, Kennedy,
Reagan, Connally, Bush, Anderson are
lit from nowhere within. "The fucks,"
my student blurted, "No one makes jokes
about them because no one gives a shit
what those fucks do." Shoeshine
on Bromfield Street and a "cold enough
for you" chat. The man still blocks
hats, has the blocks at least. In these
bareheaded days they sit featureless
blackened more loaf than skull.
There could be a Smith, a Cubi,
two blocks over and worth the walk
if the city fathers had not been
cheapskates and philistine undertakers,

parking lot owners, later to be
indicted grifters, fifteen years ago.
In Washington the huge Smiths, one
a black shield or out-thrust chest on
wheels, came out of the fog that was
tear gas and rain, came out like
ancient ornery things. We ran between
them. Grazing and littering the Monument
lawn the Smith's seemed let out and police
came through the doors of the Smithsonian
after us. February asparagus? From
California, rushing it, expensive and
fibrous I know but hard to resist.
Will one day make a difference?
To Marni and Arden mother passes on
the saga of my three "made shit
of" cars, all gifts. They pass this on to me
eagerly and smirking to let me know
how much they love knowing this about
me. The '50 Pontiac threw a rod
outside Albany on a day bitter cold
as this. It died. I carried its battery
home on the milk train seeing false dawn
a cold blue flame and the Hudson hemmed
with thrown together stacks of ice and
passed Sing Sing grim as grim
in the frigid dawn. The Plymouth
convertible went by itself, the driver
was *that* drunk, into a traffic standard
outside Parsippany, New Jersey one
moonless October a.m. And the Singer
one of a kind English car with column
shift that worked backwards in and up
for first and so on: the Singer
bucked, hood tore up and blew,
clearing the windshield, off, sparks
flew through the engine's thick oil
smoke and the car coughed, shuddered
shook me in my seat and coughed again
its last beside the road in Westfield,
New Jersey. How gray and dowdy the Boston
Transcript upper floors. Dusty windows.
No one worked here in years. The jeweler
shakes out a length of butcher paper

and smooths it to hide his wares. Father
knew men like him and I waited in stores
like his while father bought another
watch at discount, the dime thin Patek
Phillipe he didn't need that wound up
in his dresser junk drawer. This one
is no older than I, no leaner getting
his sleep flossing his teeth keeping
the wolf from the door hand on the
tiller. Oh, all gray the sky goes over
the narrow street. James Wright is
dying Russell told me. I do not know
Wright, but he has been in some way
an older brother and like an older
brother while more distant than a
father easier to pick things up from.
He is going through his papers
seeing old friends one last time
and perhaps Russell sees or I see
Wright's conduct calling us
to our own fifteen years hence
and if those fifteen years are
as dense with incident, drama, life
and so much to be forgotten
this poem at least will remind me I
was here on this day walking with
not a thing clear in mind . . .
I have liked Wright's poems, changed
my mind, been fed up with their self-
pity and self-degradation (How similiar
these are!) taught his work and failed
to see the world as the abuser that
abused him and then the flat voice,
near toneless tuneless voice of recent
poems brought me back to him. Poems
written in Italy, in France. One in a
"New Yorker" not long ago set in Nimes
and another I remember for Max Jacob
as Wright wandered in moonlight the French
trenches of W.W. I. I heard him read
once, and he called for requests at the end
but said no when a woman asked him
to read from *Shall We Gather At The River*.
"No," he said looking off to the side,

"No I won't read from that, even one."
Is that what he said? I can hear his
soft regret and see the sideways tilt
of his bearded head. So many passing
                    thoughts of death
                    and dying. Snags
                    in the stream
                    and below the
                    dimpled sucking water's
                    surface the forever
                    pull: otherworld
                    underworld. The
                    text we cannot
                    read as I set
                    forth today not
                    a whisper of death
                    in my mind, my
                    shadow behind me
                    the world set
                    like a table
                    all before me
                    clear in the day's
                    shine, sharpened
                    to glinty points
                    by the raw wind
                    whipped as it is
                    by March which
                    can do nothing
                    but come to us
                    a lion. I've taught
                    a class; made them
                    laugh; filled my
                    bag with vegetables;
                    passed the stores
                    I sometimes stop in;
                    glimpsed (mind's eye)
                    sex—sudden meaty
                    intrusions—and decided
                    to walk Boylston
                    Street home foregoing
                    windy, scouring Columbus
                    Avenue. One Clivia
                    flower is cringed
                    gone by but others

come off like bullets
from the stalk that
forces its way between
the long leaves that
usually make a fan
but are now
every which way
disarray. Two flowers
with a fist full
to bloom are open
orange trumpets
thrusting forth
furry topped pistils
from their yellow
throats. They turn
themselves to the
second floor window
for me who knows
where to look.

SUNDAY NIGHT

Can't sleep.
Close my eyes. Turn
away from heart's side
draw up right knee
cuddle to my love
who asleep turns
from me and come
to lie staring up
at the lights of
cars and street lights
intersecting with dark
stretched to vanishing
triangles whose patterns
amount to nothing much.
Hurrying click-click
high heels. Old desire:
to fall asleep awake.
Second of branch
cleft bathroom light
blackens the window.
There was a boy's
unmarked face here
smooth and thin
without the fat
of a double chin
and the white
weedy hairs that
stand out in three
day's growth of beard.
What sad brown
calf's eyes
and high forehead
with several tiny
scars around the eyebrows
knit among laugh lines
like the web
of streets on a map
read by glove compartment
light in a ghostly lit
and speeding car.
Fast because lost

and furious because
far from home
the night fog
swirls from ditches
and long grass
as frost settles
sparkling. The driver
the other's face
lit from below
by greenish dashlight
reflects as one
with white lines
disappearing into
the cave ahead
and lapped up
like bead chain
pulled. Lights out.
Starless, moon passed
cold draughts from
countless gaps, cracks
ill fit windows
curl up my legs.
Thirty year's steps
the shivering hair
there should be
sparse and white
and Sundays at heart
no less sleepless
worrying on the edge
of what edge and
no friend to tell me.

Ray's letterpoem
today mildly hungover
cottonmouthed—too many
cigarettes (Neill went
out for more!)
My nose stings
from drink or
cold? Boulder snow
flurries. Cloudless blue
sky here clean
as a plate Ray.
Basil, the dog
you've never seen
a Norfolk terrier,
sleeps at my feet
cries softly having
a dream. Last
night I dreamt
of soft, fried
mice. Scout's honor.

Crossing the Public Garden
thunk went the
workman's mattock
thunk again. "Good
joints man?" Three
black kids. The one
wearing a pearl blue
homburg. No dope
for me just beer
at noisy Jake Wirth's.
Hannigan, Harrison and
Reed surely. Yes
I recall Freeman
and Movius the two
Phd's trying to decide
if you stick
your head up your
ass (that's if you
could) would it
be possible to turn
yourself inside out?
Many drinks made
me thirsty couldn't
ask for ginger ale.
These men I knew
I no longer see.

Boston's afternoon pink
glow seems to rise
from the floor of streets.
"Clouds scared me."
What a childhood!
That's Art Pepper talking.
What a life!
Music, heroin, prison
and a moral code
based on cleanliness
and never being a "rat."
What will the fare
be for the '80's?
"A Year, A Decade"
the Revolution Books
window placard promises
"OF HISTORIC IMPORTANCE"
and right they are.
There is the food
calendar. January —
black radishes. April—leeks.
Vegetables lit erotically
some shot in soft-
focus like movie stars.
The Kliban cat calendar.
His wily cat (Wily
cat? Is that like
"He must smell
my dog on me"
when you reach to
pet a dog and
the dog sniffs you?)
waits on a tree branch
wearing a bird's beak.
And Ellen's gift
the calendar with
red earth colored
Navajo blanket patterns
above the months.

"Poetry," John Wieners
told me "is no longer
on my calendar."
John, beautiful poet
kind and formal man,
who served me creme de menthe
in gold rimmed goblets
and a plate of carrots,
shrugged and seemed relieved.

Putting socks away
or idly going
through my chest
of drawers mother
came across poems
I had hidden
there to keep
them to myself.
She had no idea
I was writing
and after her
surprise, and, I bet,
glee at turning up
anything so revealing
of my private life
she saw something
to make her proud
as she sat on the bed
and read through
the poems. I was
sixteen and away
at school.
After she read
the poems she
took them to
the local paper—
a weekly—and
got the editor
to print them
all taking up
an entire page even
a note reading (I
think I remember
correctly) "Bill's
mother says he
looks more like
a football player
than a poet."
I knew nothing

of this when
she brought the
paper to me.
It was spring
an outdoor party
of some sort
at school and
she came across
the lawn waving
the paper. Everyone
heard her cry
"Have I got
a surprise for you!"
She paused to show
the paper to
parents, my teachers
and school friends
before she reached
me, and I saw
for the first time
my name in
print, my poems
there never having
thought of them
as anything but mine
and wanting at
that exact moment
to die for shame
and disappear.

YOUTH

Russo, rimless
glasses, he
sat cross-legged
open book
held like
a hymnal
and read
Vachel Lindsay's
"The Congo."
"You boys
may not
like this
but some
of you girls
might." Drobish
played with
himself in that
class and
Johnny Bozo
always choose
South Africa's
Orange river
in the map
game. Johnny's
cousin Ray
had, so Johnny
claimed, an
enormous cock.
Ray had to
tie it to
his leg
to avoid an
incredible bulge.
Past a gas
station then
a beauty shop
up the hill
Johnny lived
on a small
all but
sold off

farm. There
was a pond
and cows
walking to
the barn.
Pitted mud
tracks around
the pond—
Pee Pond.
Skaters came
there. The half
of their bodies
toward the night's
fire red-gold
and sparks
exploding stagger
pulled up
to the stars.

READING

The lady three chairs
away yawning over
"Alfred Hitchcock's
Mystery Magazine."
Across from me
"Yankee Magazine"
held like a hand mirror.
She forgot her glasses.
Newspapers rattle. One
"Time" reader his finger
moves across the page.
A paperback thick
as the Michener novels
people read on the subway
she reads with the cover
curled under and so curls
the Barbara Cartland cover
read beside her.
Looking slyly along
my right shoulder
as if at the clock
catch the chapter heading
"Bereavement and Religion."
Stopping to light a cigarette
she turns the book face
up. *The Bereaved Parent*.
She doesn't sigh
or look sad
but would she read
such a book
if she had not
lost a child?
And me? After
the sport's page
Hymn to Life
for the, I forget,
fourth or fifth time,
and this new book
on Viennese culture
and politics (I don't
want to get caught

short) which I may
not get to before
Arden finishes
with the dentist.
Do I scratch
myself, idly twist
my hair and
pull at my
clothes the way
these other readers
do? I must.
All of us reading
twitching like insects.

WASHINGTON'S BIRTHDAY

A cast down
sword of sunlight
rests its crumpled point
on sleeping Basil
brings up his colors
wheaten and grizzle.
The clouds roll over
like milk in water.
More milk than water.
The country is far
away under nickel
browned over, snowed under
lavender hollows and red
branches like fresh scratches.
Bay State Road
enough gritty new
snow to hold
footprints. Younger, I
was here to visit
the dentist, tilted
back in his chair
and again a meeting
of angry teachers
during the war.
A man said,
"College finances are
a can of worms
they keep in the
ground." Got me
in trouble later
when I threw
the line at my
friend's father, a
lawyer, and he
nearly took my
head off. Chocolate
cake soiled the
white pants I
wore. The light
darkens around these
instant, dispatched

snapshots. Tire tracks
cross the snow
like friction tape.
There is mist
on The Castle windows.
Bob's black moustache
and goatee, his sign,
is lost in gray.
He must raise
his soft voice.
And mist there was
on the windshield
of Schwartz's Chevy
wiped off with a glove
returning from that
hockey game at Canterbury.
I sat in the death seat
flipping through Pound's
Selected Poems I had
bought mostly for show
when I came upon
the Chinese poems and
by the open glove
compartment's light I could
hardly concentrate for
the excitement I felt.
Looking down, looking up
there was a lighted
window above me clear
and *on* the dark
we passed. I did not know
nothing will be
the same. No friend
true. No love
does not change.

CROSSING BORDERS

The mailman. Gold hood.
The mailman. Cold out.
How many are there
like me sitting at
desk, unshaven, 10 a.m.
the radio on one
ear cocked for the crash
of mail through the slot?
You can't live
for yourself alone.
Oh, you can but
is that all
there is to it?
Demonstrate charm,
advertise connectedness,
know the different
cheeses, how to garden
where to travel
until the dark rises
out of the indifferent bushes.

Above the cold
snow-filling street
of the wig maker
and pen seller
Neill's Roman pink
and red clay marks
on cream paper.
Drawings pinned up
so that when
something catches his
eye he can stop
to look and tell
those that work
from those that don't.
They declare themselves
clefts, triangles and
nervous pencil lines
scoring the faded
gray air. Perfect day
for work. The snow
an aid to meditation
hastening the drowse
that is wakefulness
to one thing
entwined with many
like a cable
until you step back
look up and find
there what has been
in you a long time
now presents itself
for you to recognize.

HERB GARDEN

Working by hand,
and with pitchfork
or hoe, pulling out
two year's growth
of weeds from the herb garden.
Tenacious witch grass
and in the oregano
thyme and chives
grass and clover.
The ringing thunk
of a clean driven nail.
New house going up
on an old meadow.
Where the barn was—
nothing and only a few
blackberry canes left.
Dig and then clear
asparagus plants that came
too early for anyone.
What roots! Wigs,
interconnected wigs
of meaty pipes.
Good to work
up a sweat
feel the dirt
on my hands
wiped across my forehead.
Plant basil, a bush
of the small leaf kind,
and flat leaf parsley.
Dill and basil seed.
A new French tarragon
plant the old still
here but nearly overcome
by grass is puny.
For a border
DRURY bricks late
of the chimney
orange, brittle knocked
into place sometimes
come apart in flakes.

POSTSCRIPT

Those asparagus plants
I put in the day
after Gordon Cairnie died
as a memorial
boasting they would
last and yield
for sixty years
so my children
might be around
to pick and eat
them remembering.
In six years but
two thin stalks
the rest went to seed
after the stalks grew
tall beautifully into
lacy arrowhead ferns
so heavy they fell
into sage and chives.
Now it is Philip dead
and in the roots
I grip and tug
caught is a nail
hand forged like
those he painted
common and austere.

BEACON HILL

Not so many memories
this bright snow gusts
in squalls from Cambridge
baffling vision obscuring
the slice of river
seen coming down Pinckney St.
inside a gray bulb:
a yard long loaf
of Russian black bread
stolen, in the oven
West Cedar Street
and on Joy Street
Charlie and Julie.
They kept their "giggles"
in a tackle box
bourbon in his shirts.
He either was or
wasn't special forces Vietnam:
she insisted her mother
who drunkenly bought
the portrait of Julia Child
did with her brother . . .
among many confidences
offered in friendship
until knowing too much
poisoned intimacy.
Charlie killed his dog
with a knife and
like most students,
like Chester who gave me dope
behind a now gleaming
90 A, Charlie disappeared.
As long ago as Proulx
same as the realtor's name
Franny Proulx scrap of blond
memory he rode helicopters
out of the sky over
Vietnam and died
married to Martha.
Clear fragments. Shadows fill
narrow shuttered steep

and white streets.
The abating snow discloses
the Hill's frosted rooftops
rising in tiers like
cakes of brick
with wood palisades
and blackened chimneys
old and cozy mounting
to the state house
gold leaf dome
looked down upon
by keeps of banking
and commerce come
to their height over
seventeen winters as
the city shrinks around them.

TO HSÜCH T'AO

Each poem has its own pattern of tones.
For a long time I knew only
how to write elegies
and verse shadowed by Horatian melancholy.
at the daily passing of things.
This a drunk poet told me
when I was already gorged
on my sad one note
and sworn to shake loose
let myself go
and become a schoolboy again
for anyone to teach me
but how quickly the months pass.

TWO FOR CHARLES SIMIC

I

       Off 6th. Avenue
The distant call:
"Goin' out tonight
Hey, youuu . . ."
From . . . From where?
Above! High above.
The women prisoners
calling through the bars
most of their voices lost
and dropping messages
on strings like spiders
to waiting pimps and lovers
who look heavenward.

II

Attila rode under
such a crow
who roused the crickets
and brings the frost
who shreds the air
with his call
and where he roosts
he leaves the tree red,
His bitten shadow
passes over this page:
the man, often arrested
and sent to Billerica
for handing out
little pictures of the saints
at defense plant gates,
is dead at twenty-four.

Return to the same address
gaunt brick bound streets
four block walk for groceries
the bus to Cambridge
rolling like a ball bearing
in its worn groove
all the time wanting
Vermont's bare architecture
clapboards, cedar pillared walks
and an art ruled
by straightedge and hawk's eye
and to live in cities
of ochre stone arches
wine tasting of herbs
gardens to the sea
and wide shade to drowse in.
To be anonymous—
all eyes, all ears and nerves.

VERMONT APOLLINAIRE

"From America comes the little humming-bird"
From morning mistcloud a raven descends
First the one kingfisher, plop then the mate, plop
They whirr and rattle away crossed wires
August's end tomatoes take on orange swallows disappear
The loons cry their bearded cry
Jane calls a crane stands at the stream's mouth
Stands impervious to any order save its own
From the sea mountains distant come gulls

I cannot carry a tune
Not in a bucket one note
I carry the past like a mailman letters
The past like a wave breaking always
Always about to break never in the right place
When I reach my address letters fall through the slot

The little car, the bug is yellow
1st September 2 a.m. doused with dew
now crossing the Pepperpot bridge a wind
              roughens the dark water
whipping up tiny waves. Chalk on slate.
              My shirt is plastered
to me. The joggers jog their hair
              in flames. The wind
is ringing down the last
              blossoms all over town.
Gutters are dusty with doll
              bells on stems and
on Commonwealth and Beacon pink
              magnolia petals smear
grainy rust over concrete.
              This narrow way leads
to Kendall Square where every walker
              is rearranged
by winds that sluice between new
              high rises sweeping
grit off cheerless vast plazas.
              The subway teeters by
rain like beebee chain on its many windows.
              A yellow street sweeper

below moves through the lanes
                of the cloverleaf
an ear really of highway that keeps
                to the river.
From here the state house is a gold
                thimble or nipple
swaggered over by stony giants
                blunt as stony fingers.

Summer swallows spring and goes into September
Like long division it is always there
Autumn, fall we say, fruit releases itself
You are new enough so the old catches up
Cross this bridge come to that one
You grow up and ancient history snaps back
Rubber band and rake handle

Morning before morning
Mist like flour
Cat wants in, butts the door
At garden's edge stand blackest ravens
This is the void some two or three there
Just beyond reach and they too hear cow's bell
How far that sound travels unheeded, feather on water

Humming-birds need not prepare
They know, they know their way above the clouds
from this red sugar water all the way to Mexico

Goodbye Goodbye
You ruby throats who stop in air

Memory ardent for mercy